"*Powerful Educator* is the inspiration and action guide in our work opening a new school these last three years. As a team, we continue to reflect and improve on our teaching practice using these important principles in serving ALL our students and ensuring Equity and Excellence for ALL."

Merrill Mathews, *Principal, Irma Coulson Public School*

"The ingredients of any terrific school in the world are great teaching and more of it. For teachers truly to be great, they are not just masters of imparting academic knowledge and skills; they are also great at building relationships with their students and building a culture of comfortable high expectations and nurturing family in their classrooms. Mawi's *Powerful Educator* helps teachers learn what to do after the lesson plans are done to ensure they are set up for success and setting up their students for success."

—Mike Feinberg, *Co-Founder, KIPP Schools*

"In *Powerful Educator,* Mawi provides a powerful framework for helping educators and parents capitalize on the tremendous potential we have to impact the lives of young people. Through inspiring stories from his own remarkable childhood, experiences of the many youth and educators he has worked with, and lessons from the literature on character development and motivation, Mawi provides concrete and inspiring examples of the incredible impact that small, but deliberate, actions by caring adults can have on the life outcomes of youth."

—Johanna Even, *Director of the Improving Schools Initiative, EdVestors*

DEDICATION

Dedicated to Powerful Educators around the world.

ACKNOWLEDGMENTS

Many thanks to all the schools and families that have allowed me to learn with them the last fifteen years. Special thanks to Allison Niebauer and Pat Donohue for their editing of this book; and to Derek Murphy and Victor Kore for their design.

Published by Mawi Learning.
www.MawiLearning.com

Asgedom, Mawi.
POWERFUL EDUCATOR:
How to Inspire Student Growth

ISBN 978-0-9860772-1-0

Cover design by Derek Murphy.
Interior design and layout by Victor Kore.
Cover image provided by smarnad and Bigstock.

Quantity discounts are available on bulk purchases. For more information, please email **info@mawilearning.com**

POWERFUL EDUCATOR™

POWERFUL
EDUCATOR™

How to Inspire Student Growth

MAWI ASGEDOM

CONTENTS

INTRODUCTION

O ver the last 14 years, I've had the privilege of working with thousands of educators across the world. I've been humbled by the challenges they face. Here are some of the stories educators have shared:

Our school is so competitive that many of the kids are on anxiety medication. The parents will tell you that they want their kid to be happy, but really, they want their kid to attend an Ivy League School.

My school has had eight principals in four years. I spend so much energy on adults I have little left over for my students. I'm tired of new initiatives. I'm tired of new leaders. I'm just tired.

98% of the kids at my school are on free and reduced lunches. I try to teach but most of the time I'm just playing policeman.

Parents have also shared their own challenges:

My daughter has been bullied for years. I met with the principal and the superintendent and it didn't help - it seems the school has no power to combat verbal abuse. Even though we will lose $150,000, we have put our house on the market. Our daughter cannot survive another year here.

My son cares more about reality shows and pop stars than anything I have to say. His priorities are: his friends, his girlfriend, and his phone.

Ever since my divorce, my daughter has tuned out. She used to be a good student, but has had C's and D's the last year. I'm not around as much as I'd like because I have to work overtime.

Challenges like these can make any adult feel powerless. Especially because we know there are no silver bullets. No magic buttons we can press to instantly and permanently fix these problems.

Where is the Power?

When I first started working with schools, I worked almost exclusively with students. I did a few parent and educator presentations but over 90% of my work was with students. The reason was simple. I believed that I could inspire any student with my life story.

At age six, I came to the United States as a refugee from war-torn Ethiopia. I did not know any English and grew up on welfare and in low-income housing. Fifteen years later, I graduated from Harvard University.

Through my story, I wanted students to see that anyone of any background could live the American Dream. And today, I still have deep belief in the power that our students have to create opportunity. But after working with over 1,000,000 students and observing every kind of school possible, I believe the greatest power lies with us, with adults.

As educators and parents, we create the world that students live in - we create the families, the schools, and the communities. We create the mindsets and expectations. To inspire our youth, we need to believe in our own power and use that power continuously. Even when we feel tired and question our impact. Even when we face intractable challenges.

This book unabashedly asserts that you - as an educator,

parent, relative, or community member - have the power to profoundly impact youth. In this book, I will show you how to use your five most foundational powers.

Who is a Powerful Educator?

WHEN I WAS IN MIDDLE SCHOOL, I used to go shopping at a local grocery store called Jewel. Well, shopping is the wrong word. Several friends and I would enter Jewel and after some quick surveillance, head for the baseball card section. My friends preferred TOPPs but my favorite cards were Donrus, and the dream card was the Ken Griffey Junior card. The Griffey Jr. was rumored to be worth $70.[1]

There was only one problem. My annual budget was roughly three dollars, consisting primarily of money I found on the sidewalk as I walked back and forth to school. One pack of baseball cards cost 50 cents.

In the store, I would open my empty backpack. After a few furtive glances, I would quickly load three cartons of Donrus. Each carton had 36 packs and each pack had 15 cards. So in one trip, I would steal 1,620 cards. Sometimes, I made 3 trips in one day, totaling 4,860 cards. We stole so many cards one summer that the store had to install a glass security system, where you could buy baseball cards only if a store employee unlocked them with a key.

---

1. The two dominant baseball card brands at the time were TOPPS and Donrus. TOPPs was the traditional, affordable brand with history that went back decades. Donrus was newer and a little flashier.

Sometimes I wonder what would have happened if I had been caught - assuming my father let me live. Would I have been sent to "Juvie" or Juvenile Detention? As a low-income black boy with a record, would I have been permanently labeled a low-potential kid? Would I have gone down a drastically different path than a scholarship to Harvard?

My best friend and frequent partner in crime was my older brother Tewolde. But as he entered his sophomore year of high school, my brother changed. Tewolde stopped stealing; he worked harder in his classes; he even started his own cleaning business to make money for my family. Tewolde's transformation was driven by an increased desire to care for our family and by his spiritual growth.

I kept shoplifting with friends from my middle school, until my brother did the unthinkable. He sat me down and told me that if he ever heard that I was stealing again, he would tell our dad about our shoplifting over the last few years. Telling my dad was the nuclear option. As my siblings often say, in our family, there were no "Time Outs," only "Knock You Outs." I never shoplifted again.

My life changed forever during my sophomore year, and my brother's senior year. Tewolde went on a road trip, and about 3:00 AM, a drunk driver slammed into his car, killing Tewolde instantly.

That horrific week, as I went through my brother's desk, I discovered something that inspires me to this day. A 6-year old child's photo. My brother had been paying $20/month to sponsor a child across the world, providing that child with food and an education. *The kid who had shoplifted just years before now used money he got from cleaning bathrooms to save a child's life.*

Tewolde helped me understand the answer to an important question: Who is a Powerful Educator? Is it a parent, a grandparent, a coach, counselor, a teacher? Yes. But it is also the older brother or sister; it is a neighbor or college student. A Powerful Educator is anyone who loves youth, believes in youth, and takes action to help youth grow.

Let's take a closer look at why our youth need Powerful Educators.

The Story All Cultures Tell

IN THE RURAL ETHIOPIAN VILLAGE where I was born, almost no one could read. For example, my own mother couldn't read in any language before she came to the United States.

Lacking literacy, Ethiopian villagers used a powerful method to pass on wisdom from one generation to the next. **Stories**. Like the ancient Greeks before and countless other cultures since, Ethiopian villagers told stories.

For example, one of my favorite Ethiopian stories is of the blind man who carried a lantern around at night. When people asked him why a blind man needs light, he told them the light was not for himself, but for them. I first heard this story in the refugee camp, and it has stuck with me ever since.

We all have our own favorite stories. In this book, I will ask you to consider your role in what is often called "the great story."

Joseph Campbell was a renowned anthropologist and psychologist who spent his career studying how cultures create stories. Through his decades of research, Campbell demonstrated that all human cultures tell the same basic "great story," with the same archetypal characters and plotline.

- **THE HERO:** The great story features a young hero of humble means. Orphans such as Harry Potter, Luke Skywalker, and King Arthur are great examples.
- **THE EVILDOER:** An evil character threatens the entire land. For example, Voldemort in Harry Potter or The Emperor in Star Wars.
- **THE MENTOR:** There is always a mentor that provides wisdom, training, and support. Dumbledore counsels Harry Potter; Yoda trains Luke Skywalker; Merlin advises King Arthur.

This great story has been told thousands of ways, and it encapsulates the collective wisdom of cultures across the world. The only thing that has changed for the better, is that the hero is now as likely to be a heroine.

Our Heroic Story

IN THE GREAT STORY OF how we raise our youth, the characters are both different and the same:

- **The Hero:** Our youth, of all socioeconomic backgrounds, can contribute in incredible ways to our world. They have vast power, but will they realize it?

- **The Evildoer:** The personal challenges our heroes might face, such as poverty, illness, and family problems. The larger, macro challenges our world faces such as war and disease. Can our heroes defeat the Evildoer?
- **The Mentor:** This is you. Without your guidance, love, and support, the hero will fail. Without the guidance of parents, mentors, and educators, the Evildoer will destroy our youth.

I could try to convince you of the power of educators and parents by giving you research studies and data sets. And I do provide studies in Appendix A that show how critical parents and educators are.

But you don't need the research. You know intuitively, without the data, that educators matter. That parents matter. That caring adults matter. You know that our youth have as much chance of reaching greatness on their own as Luke Skywalker had of unlocking the Force without Yoda.

That's why you matter and why you can never give up, regardless of the challenges your school or family faces; even if you feel like you have nothing to add, or your home is in shambles, or your school is falling apart.

Heroic stories are impossible without you. Our youth need you to say, "Yes. I will embrace my power. I will train you. I will challenge you. I will help you see that you have far more in you than you ever thought."

The Five Powers of An Educator

YOU HAVE COUNTLESS WAYS THAT you can inspire and impact youth. In this book, I will train you to use five of your foundational powers. Each of these Five Powers has its own chapter:

1. **Press Your Turbo Button**
2. **Relate With Heart**
3. **Speak Success Mindsets**
4. **Push for Skill**
5. **Champion Voice**

Why did I pick these five? After all, you have endless ways that you can impact youth. I based The Five Powers on:

- Field work with schools: I have worked directly with over 1,000 schools, where I have visited the school in person, met the administrators, and worked with students and teachers. This book is driven primarily by what tens of thousands of educators and 1,000,000+ students have taught me over the last fifteen years.

- Success Literature & Research: I've studied the research on youth development and interviewed many leading researchers such as Stanford University professor Dr. Carol Dweck, who pioneered the Growth Mindset. These Five Powers blend the work of leading researchers with our society's collective wisdom on youth success. In Appendix B, I share some of this research.

- Personal experience: I came to this country as a refugee from Ethiopia and lived the American Dream because of Powerful Educators such as my parents, teachers, and coaches. My own story shows me that no student, however motivated, can rise to their best without Powerful Educators.

How to Use This Book

If I meet you at the airport someday and you tell me that you read this book, and perhaps that you liked it, I will thank you. If you can tell me something that you DID as a result of reading this book, I will buy you a sandwich. I really will.[2]

Action is the bridge between training and impact, and I challenge you to read this book with an eye for how you can apply it.

I recommend first just reading this book and absorbing the main ideas. Perhaps a specific story will jump out at you. Maybe one of the Five Powers will resonate with your current circumstances.

Then start applying it. You can do it however you want. You can make a list of things that you can do immediately; you can focus on one Power at a time; you can create a detailed plan. To help you, each chapter ends with questions and discussion points you can use to apply the Five Powers to your own situation.

---

2. Limit: Mawi buys three sandwiches a day. I will not buy sandwiches for your entire school if I meet 100 of you at the airport.

If you are on a school team, you might evaluate your school on the Five Powers and strategically work on one. For example, I recently worked with a team of 30 principals from a large urban district and they identified Power #5, Champion Voice, as their greatest focus for the coming year.

Extend Your Lantern

As you get into the details of the Five Powers, remember the larger story. Our youth need you. They need you to be a coach, parent, mentor, teacher, uncle, aunt, administrator. They need you to embrace your role in the Great Story and become the Powerful Educator you are meant to be.

Being a Powerful Educator does not mean you will always feel powerful. Nor does it mean you will always know what to do. More often than not, you may feel like the blind man with the lantern, stumbling around at night.

Like him, extend your light anyway.

─────────────────────POWER 1
Press Your Turbo Button

In his mega bestseller, *The Seven Habits of Highly Effective People,* Stephen Covey makes a startling claim. Dr. Covey writes that the person who takes action has **5,000 times the power** of the person who does not take action.

Is Dr. Covey right? As an educator or parent, can you access 5,000 times the power simply by taking action?

How to Get on Oprah without a Publicist

WHEN I WAS 23 YEARS old, I was just starting my writing and speaking career. I had self-published my first book, *Of Beetles and Angels: A Boy's Remarkable Journey from a Refugee Camp to Harvard.*

Almost every week, a different friend told me that I should try to get on the Oprah Winfrey Show. At that time, Oprah's show was legendary for its reach and "Midas" touch for authors lucky enough to be interviewed.

There was only one problem. Actually a whole host of problems. I had no publicist and no connection to Oprah. Oprah did not book self-published authors. And there were a gazillion other authors trying to get on the show.

I took the one action I could. I went to Oprah's website and found the page with the comment box. I sent the link to all my newsletter readers and asked them to tell Oprah why my story was a good fit for her show.

I believe even Dr. Covey would have been shocked by the results of this small action.

- The next year, Oprah had me on her show and her producers told me it was because of the comment box campaign.
- When the show called me, I was in the final stages of selling my memoir to a major publisher. The publisher substantially increased their offer after hearing I would go on Oprah's show.
- Oprah went on to name the show one of the 20 best shows of her entire career.

Because I sent out that one website link, my ability to reach students skyrocketed and I entered a whole new phase in my career.

The Turbo Button™

ABOUT TEN YEARS AGO, I was playing video games with my brother Hntsa and Hntsa was smoking me. We played basketball and he beat me 87-10. We played football and he intercepted everything, sacking me at will, blowing me out by scores like 56-7.

I had played video games for years. How could Hntsa trounce me so thoroughly?

When I asked Hntsa, he started laughing. Then he turned his controller upside down. *There was a secret button underneath the joystick!* This button was called the Turbo Button.

The Turbo Button gave a player extra speed, power, and juice. All you had to do was press it. But I couldn't press it because I didn't know it existed.

Just like there is a Turbo Button on a joystick, I believe that all of us have a Turbo Button in our hearts. We press this button anytime we take action to improve our lives.

Pressing the Turbo Button can be small, like sending out one email to a newsletter list. Or it can be big, like completing a doctorate degree.

Here are some simple examples of parents and educators pressing their Turbo buttons:

- The dad who reads to his kids for 10 minutes each day.
- The librarian that sets aside a book she knows a particular student will enjoy.
- The teacher who takes an extra five minutes to create a game she knows will enliven a lesson.

When that dad reads to his child, that dad is accepting his power to be a difference maker and change agent in his child's life. Reading that book seems like a small action, but it actually puts that dad in a separate category of impact that has 5,000 times the power.

Turbo Drums

SEVERAL YEARS AGO I SPOKE at a middle school in Alameda, California. It was a low-income school with a predominantly minority population.

I met a security guard there named Lester. A few years earlier, Lester had noticed that the students didn't have many activities, but they enjoyed drumming.

Lester wrote letters to local organizations asking them if they had any drums they could donate. He also had the kids help him raise money to purchase new drums. By the time I visited the school, they had hundreds of drums in an incredible room filled top to bottom. The school's drumline became a core part of its culture, and the kids beamed with pride, as did Lester.

Is that 5,000 times more powerful? To go from "the kids have no activities" to "we have one of the top drumlines in our area, with hundreds of drums."

Lester is not the superintendent, principal, teacher or part of the instructional team. He's a security guard. And that's what I find most inspiring. Turbo has nothing to do with our titles and everything to do with the way we view ourselves and the impact we choose to have.

Bring out the Parents!

SCHOOLS KNOW THAT PARENT ENGAGEMENT drives student success. And schools try to engage parents - they have parent nights, parent-teacher conferences, and communicate regularly through letters, emails, and these days, even text messages.

But what if the parents do not come to your events? What if you've tried everything, and at your school of 1,500 students, only 20 parents show up to your events?

Such was the situation at a high school I worked with in Central Washington. 80% of the students were Hispanic, many of them recent immigrants. The parents often worked several jobs and could not get off work. Cultural and language barriers also prevented parents from attending school events.

A teacher named David Rodriguez noticed that some of his English language students loved to tell jokes. David worked with these students to write an entertaining telenovela-type play completely in Spanish. The play included many asides about what parents could do to help their student succeed. For example, the play dramatized how damaging it was academically when parents took their kids back to Mexico for a month in the middle of the school year, a common practice at the school.

The students handled everything. They performed the entire play. They marketed it to the parents. *In its third year over 500 parents attended! Parent night went from a few scattered rows to a standing room only crowd.*

One educator, with one idea, directed at a chronic challenge, was able to drive unimagined results by hitting his Turbo Button.

Resist the temptation to think: *Well, that was just David. I can't write a play like that. Just because it worked there does not mean it will work here.*

Powerful educators say: *That's yet another example of the power all of us have. And while I may not have the same challenges, or get the same results, I can hit my Turbo Button in my own way.*

Turbo, not Extrovert

AFTER MY SOPHOMORE YEAR IN college, I ran a summer school for elementary age students. I had four Harvard undergraduates on my staff, along with several other college students.

One of the staff members, Michael, was about the most outgoing person you could meet. He had a ready smile for everyone and quickly got to know everyone. But I had to fire Michael two weeks into the summer for violating staff rules.

Another staff member, Des, smiled a lot less and he certainly never hugged anyone. But Des:

- Mopped the floor every day after lunch. I never asked Des to do this - he just volunteered.
- Planned his lessons meticulously ahead of time.
- Established deep relationships with the parents of the students, even visiting their homes.

Turbo does not mean extrovert. Turbo means you take action. You initiate. Your proactivity makes your school and your family better.

Me Turbo & We Turbo

WHEN YOU PRESS YOUR Turbo Button, you often do so within a system such as a family, a business, or a school district. Consider this chart that explains the difference between Me Turbo and We Turbo.

	Me Turbo	We Turbo
Team	I can do this now.	I need to build support for this.
Success	My students got amazing results.	Our school got amazing results.
Politics	As long as I help students, nothing matters.	I am a part of a district that helps kids.

Powerful Educators attune themselves to both types of Turbo. For example, let's consider this true story of Megan, a middle school teacher in Illinois.

One day, Megan read in the local paper that food banks in the county had run out of food, and many families were being turned away.

So Megan hit her Turbo Button. She recruited twenty students to do a food drive and posted signs across the school. In just two weeks, her students collected over 1200 cans. Megan's class received a service award from the local Food Bank. The local paper also ran an article celebrating the students' impact and their award.

The next week Megan overheard some of her colleagues discussing the food drive. Here are some of the things she heard:

- "Megan always has to be in the spotlight."
- "Aren't we doing our annual food drive next month?"
- "Megan is the #1 buttkisser in the district. I've been telling you that for years."

What happened? How could a food drive for the needy turn into vitriolic gossip?

Rock The Boat

MEGAN USED HER ME TURBO without using enough We Turbo. We Turbo might have done the following:

- Recruited two other teachers and an administrator to support the drive.
- Connected her drive to the annual food drive.
- Focused the newspaper article on the school's existing food drive and the other teachers running it.

Megan was not trying to get credit for herself. Nor was she trying to "steal the spotlight." Unfortunately, her colleagues interpreted her Turbo as a threat.

If you've been around schools long enough, you've heard the expression, "Don't rock the boat." That's another way of saying "Don't use your Turbo." Stories like Megan's are the reason why.

As a Powerful Educator, you will often rock the boat. When you do, use both Me and We Turbo, and remember what Harry Truman said, "It is amazing what you can accomplish if you do not care who gets the *credit*."

Credit is the oil that makes Turbo go around at many schools. **The more amazing your results, the more amazing you have to be at giving others credit.**

Even if you did everything yourself, here is what you should say, "None of this would be possible without a supportive administration. Listen, you really should be talking to my colleagues, not me. I couldn't do anything without them. When you have such supportive parents, everything is easy."

Your Turbo Button Only

I'VE KNOWN SAM AND JENNY for twelve years. If there was such a thing as "perfect" parents, I'd say it's them. Jenny followed all the scientific best practices: from taking prenatal vitamins, to not drinking Diet Coke during her pregnancy, to nursing for a year.

Sam and Jenny read every day to their children, did their best to teach responsibility and character to their kids, and yet when their oldest, Bruce, was in high school, he was the most apathetic student you could imagine.

Bruce got D's his first two years of high school. He was caught smoking and drinking on multiple occasions. Counseling sessions yielded no change. Escalating systems of accountability and consequences had no impact. Nothing "worked."

The Turbo Button is both empowering and limiting. Empowering because you can always press your own Turbo Button. *Limiting because you can never press anyone else's, no matter how much you love that person.*

An educator can do their best to create a stimulating, nurturing, and challenging environment. But the educator cannot enter their students' hearts and press that Turbo button for them.

Parents like Sam and Jenny can pour out endless love to their kids. But they cannot enter their children's hearts and press their Turbo Button.

As painful as it may seem, we are not meant to press each other's Turbo Buttons. The most basic right and power of any human being is their power to choose when and how they will act.

Bruce's Story

So what did Sam and Jenny do? And what happened to their son Bruce?

Sam and Jenny hit their Turbo Buttons in the following ways:

- **Grace:** They gave each other grace. Grace means no blame game. No second guessing of past parenting: *You were too hard on him. You were too easy on him.*
- **Acceptance:** In their heads, they had envisioned a dif-

ferent high school career for Bruce. They accepted the reality that their son would barely graduate.

- **Release:** They accepted that they could not control their son's actions. That at some level, it was not about finding the right intervention.

Grace meant that their marriage could survive. Acceptance meant that they could adjust to best help themselves and their son. Release meant that they no longer spent every moment trying to figure out what to do next.

Note that Grace, Acceptance, and Release are all mental decisions - as opposed to external actions such as finding a new program or treatment plan. Quite often, hitting our Turbo Buttons means choosing to think differently about ourselves and our kids.

Today, Bruce is a student at a community college. He lives at home. *And that does not make him a failure.* Part of the problem is that as parents, we tell ourselves things such as: *If my son lives at home and attends community college, he failed. I failed. We are failures.*

Nothing could be further from the truth. Power 3 will train you to use the following definitions of failure and success. *Failure is when I do nothing to grow. Success is any time I try to grow.* On any day, Bruce can succeed simply by attempting to grow.

It's natural for parents to consider the toll of "lost years" or "irreversible consequences." And as a parent of three kids, trust me, I have the same fears any parent does.

But do not despair. The human being who does decide to press their Turbo Button wields an incredible "5000" times the power at any age.

And my observation from working with families for the last fifteen years is that things often work out given enough time. We want our kids to hit their Turbo Button NOW. But our kids may not be ready now; they may not hit it until they are 17, or 19, or 23.

While you may not see the immediate effects of your love and Turbo, do not lose hope. Keep planting seeds. The seeds many not bloom exactly when and how you want, but they will bloom.

The Other Button

If the Turbo Button is so powerful, how come we don't press it more often?

Because the Turbo Button is not our only option. There is another button that is bigger and much easier to hit.

When I was 22, I was writing my first book, *Of Beetles and Angels*. I only had 10 pages to go when the unthinkable happened. A thief broke into my apartment in Chicago, and stole my computer and all the back-up files for the book!

I can assure you I did not feel like hitting my Turbo Button. Instead, I had thoughts like this:

- How could this happen to me?
- There's no way I can rewrite 150 pages.
- I wish I could get my hands on that thief. I'm so angry right now.

Forget about Turbo! All I could see was my Victim Button.

The Victim Button removes our power to act and robs us of agency. It is the opposite of the Turbo Button.

Here is what Victim Language looks like:

- I could do better in Math, but the teacher doesn't like me.
- The parents in my school don't get involved - that's why our scores are so low.
- My principal is the worst manager in the world.

When we face challenges, the Victim Button can feel like a natural reaction. After all, we all need time to mourn a disappointment or to vent.

But often, we stay stuck in Victim mode for far too long, and our Victim Buttons make a bad situation worse. For example, I could complain endlessly about the thief who stole my computer, but how would that help me get my book back?

As painful as it was to lose my book, I realized that I could still hit my Turbo Button. *I could rewrite the entire book, page by page.*

I could not know at the time that Oprah Winfrey, *The Chicago Tribune, Harvard Magazine* and many other media would feature *Of Beetles and Angels* within two years of publishing. I could not know that the book would sell over 250,000 copies and be read in thousand of classrooms.

I wish I could tell you that I always hit my Turbo Button, that I always choose to "rewrite the book." But the truth is that I've hit my Victim Button many times. I've blamed friends, teachers, and bosses, instead of asking what I could do. I've assumed I was powerless, when really my Turbo Button was right there. Fortunately with *Of Beetles and Angels,* I chose Turbo over Victim.

Can you think of a time when you chose to hit your Turbo and you accomplished something important to you? Is your Victim Button currently preventing you from growing in an important way?

Turbo Leaders

I OFTEN SAY BEING A SCHOOL PRINCIPAL is the hardest job in America. Why? Because principals have to serve so many diverse stakeholders: students, staff, parents, local school board, administration. Most principals I know work 80+ hours a week and often have scant time for their own families.

This last summer, I spoke to a group of principals who faced even bigger challenges than usual. I keynoted to all 600 principals in the Chicago Public Schools. Their challenges included:

- Massive budget shortfalls: there were 1400 layoffs the week that I spoke, almost 4% of staff across the district. More cuts loomed.
- Violence: The weekend after I spoke, 14 people in Chicago were killed in gun violence, and over 82 were shot.
- Politics: A recent strike and ongoing acrimony had strained relations between the teacher's union and the administration.

I told the principals: You have so many real reasons to hit the Victim Button. But if you as the principal and leader retreat into Victim mode, if you lead Victim conversations about the budget or anything else, you will give everyone else in your school permission to hit their Victim Button.

Isn't it the same with you?

If you, as a parent, hit your Victim Button in front of your kids, how will they learn to hit their Turbo Button?

If you, as a teacher, complain about the lack of air conditioning in the building, won't the students do the same thing?

If you, as head of the school board, constantly dwell on what is wrong, won't that rob the board of its power to lead and innovate?

To their credit, I can say that the principals in the Chicago Public Schools chose Turbo over Victim. In follow-up conversations and emails, they universally said, "Yes! I am here to lead on behalf of children! *And just because things are hard, does not mean I will choose Victim over Turbo.*"

Get Married & Reduce Your Tax Bill

You can press the Turbo Button in any area of your life, not just in your work with youth. For example, consider these two true stories of people I know who created startling results in their personal lives.

Sandy was in a coffee shop when she did something she had never done before. On a piece of paper, she scrawled her name and phone number. She walked over to where my friend Luke was sitting, smacked the note on his table, and said, "Call me, I want to go out." She left before Luke could respond.

Today, Luke and Sandy are married and have two kids. I went to the wedding! How is that for hitting your Turbo Button?

My good friend Matt saw that the property tax payments on his new house would eat away all of his disposable income. He attended a free seminar at the local library on how to lower property taxes.

Then Matt hit his Turbo Button. He drove to the county assessor's office. When he entered the office, he did the opposite of what the assessor expected: Matt asked to have his taxes raised.

That really cracked up the assessor. *They reviewed his files for three minutes and then lowered his taxes by 28%!*

Let's do the math. Matt's taxes went down by $3,000 each year. A simple finance trick to figure out the lifetime value of that $3,000 as it compounds year after year is to divide $3,000 by .05. That adds up to $60,000.

Matt spent 90 minutes total lowering his taxes, the 1-hour seminar at the library plus a half hour at the assessor's office.

What if Matt would have stayed home during those 90 minutes and just complained to his wife? *He would have lost $60,000.* How about you? What will you miss out on if you do not hit your Turbo Button?

Accepting the power of The Turbo Button is not limited to your impact on youth. It's a decision to embrace each day the power you have to act. Whether to be a better father or mother, a better educator, a better community member, it's all the same, you really can live with 5,000 times the power.

Power Time

1. Name one time when you hit your Turbo Button. What were the results?
2. What comes most natural to you: Me Turbo or We Turbo? Why? Do you show patience for people who do not share your Turbo style?
3. Is there something you need to change about how you view your own children? Anything you need to accept? Anything you need to release? How do you define their success and failure?
4. What is one way that you can hit your Turbo Button this week?

POWER 2
Relate With Heart

IN THE BESTSELLING FANTASY SERIES Harry Potter is an orphan boy who has to somehow defeat Voldemort, the most evil and powerful wizard the world has ever known. In our own world, we might liken Harry's matchup to that of a first grader battling an Olympic kickboxer.

As the story goes, Harry Potter survives continuous direct attacks on his life through the aid of a mysterious power. That power, it turns out, is the love of Harry's mother who herself was killed by Voldemort when Harry was just an infant. As she was dying, Harry's mother marked Harry with her love, providing a protective force field that would last a lifetime.

At first glance, Harry's story seems just that, a story. After all, in real life, there is no such thing as a protective force field. Or is there? What if you as an adult had vast, almost mystical power that came simply from how you connected to the youth in your life?

What is Poverty?

SEVEN YEARS AGO, I SPOKE at a correctional facility for teens. The students had read my first book, *Of Beetles and Angels*, which tells my life story.

After my presentation, one of the students raised his hand and said: *"I know you lived in a refugee camp and had to adjust to the United States. But I still think our story is tougher for one reason: You had parents and teachers who supported and encouraged you. Few of us in this jail did. I'd rather be a refugee with guidance and love than a native born citizen of the United States without any support."*

It was a stunning statement. We are used to thinking of poverty in material terms, with a refugee camp being at the far end of the poverty spectrum. But here was this incarcerated teenager presenting his own compelling definition. **Poverty is the absence of positive relationships.**

Millennia ago, Aristotle said, "Without friends no one would choose to live, *though he had all other goods.*" Today, this student says, "Without Powerful Educators, none of us can succeed, even in the world's most prosperous country."

Worst Year

MY FRESHMEN YEAR AT HARVARD was perhaps the best year of my life. I played my favorite sport, pickup basketball, five times a week; I had an A average in my classes; I made countless new friends from all over the world.

Then came my sophomore year. On the first day, my computer's hard drive broke. My relationship with my roommate crumbled. I had a searing encounter with a professor that to this day makes my blood boil.

Then, one morning, a startling thought pierced my soul: *I didn't believe in God anymore.* More than anything else, my faith had anchored and inspired me through life's challenges, particularly during high school.

After surviving a refugee camp and the loss of my dear brother; after fulfilling my educational dreams with a full-tuition scholarship to Harvard; after a thrilling freshmen year, I was ready to drop out. I saw no purpose in life itself, much less Harvard. These were the kinds of thoughts that circulated through my mind endlessly: *If my body consists of a set of random atoms that form molecules, what's the difference between me and the table in my room. If I'm just like the table, what's the point of me being here?*

One thing kept me going during this depressing year- relationships. The love of everyone who had contributed to my life held me together: my parents, siblings, coaches, teachers and my guidance counselor, my Ethiopian and Eritrean community, my friends at Harvard.

I have found in my own life that Harry Potter's story is more than fantasy. I have no doubt that when you love and support a young person, you are creating a force field that will stay forever in their soul. You are creating an inner fortress, deep within their heart's castle. *Who knows when that young person will call upon you and survive because of you?*

Who Can Relate?

THE POWER OF RELATIONSHIPS IS more than feel good stories. Thought leaders in education, such as Dewey and Vygotsky, have long ago demonstrated that learning is social. Researchers have demonstrated that when students feel connected, student have increased motivation and perseverance. In Appendix B, you can find summaries of some of this research.

But how do you do it? How do you build relationships with youth?

Let's start by thinking about something else: public speaking. Many people cite public speaking as their greatest fear. In some surveys, public speaking is ranked even higher than DEATH.

To anyone anxious about speaking, Dale Carnegie gives the very best advice. Dale Carnegie is the author of the bestselling book, *How to Win Friends and Influence People*, and also the namesake of the Dale Carnegie Institute.

Carnegie's method is simple: **Speak from the heart.** Carnegie claims that someone like my mother, who speaks in broken English, can give a world-class speech if she speaks from the heart. And someone with flawless English will give a flat speech if spoken without authenticity.

Relating to kids is the same way. Youth have a "fakeness" detector that can ferret out inauthentic adults. So you could be a great athlete, physically attractive, a great musician and if you are fake, students will not relate to you.

But you could be of a different race, age, and "uncool," and if youth see that you genuinely care about and believe in them, they will give you a chance.

If you are a white man in his sixties and you are working with Mexican immigrants, do not doubt for a second that you can connect with them. If you are a black woman in your forties, you absolutely can forge a strong relationship with young Jewish girls.

Of course, cultural training and having sensitivity about people's backgrounds will always matter, just like platform skills and content organization matter for public speaking.

But nothing, nothing, nothing matters more than your genuine love for the students in your life - whether they be your children, mentees, or students.

Values Diversity

A POWERFUL EDUCATOR NAMED MRS. Morgan accomplished something close to impossible. During high school, my sister Mehret decided she wanted to join the cheerleading team. Consider these facts about my father:

- He believed dating was an American wickedness. He and my mother had gotten married by arrangement and he wanted the same for his kids.
- He refused to let his kids date or attend any high school dances.
- He would not let my sister join activities at school for fear she would develop a relationship with a boy.

My sister, a cheerleader? It was a joke. My father wouldn't let

Mehret join the debate team, much less prance around in skimpy outfits before sex-crazed teenaged boys.

Mrs. Morgan coached the cheerleading team and served as the security guard at our high school. One afternoon, Mrs. Morgan came to my house to talk to my father.

Mrs. Morgan started with a question, "Can you help me understand why Mehret cannot join the cheerleading team?"

To understand what happened next, take a look at this chart, which I openly admit relies on generalizations that cannot be applied universally.

Values Diversity		
Value	**Dominant Culture in U.S.**	**Dominant Culture in Ethiopia**
Openness	Share anything all the time	The wise keep their mouths shut
Freedom	Do what you want	Do what the elders and culture want
Control	Will stop growth	Will protect and guide

What made my family different? Certainly, our clothes, our language, our skin color, and our foods were different. But what really mattered was how we defined values such as Openness, Freedom, and Control. In the U.S., people generally define Freedom as doing what you want. In what seems like an oxymoron, my culture defines freedom as doing what others - your elders and culture - want.

In the U.S., most people believe that too much control will stifle their children's growth. In my culture, control will protect and guide, especially girls. By preventing my sister from joining the team, my father was protecting her and guiding her.

How did Mrs. Morgan accomplish the impossible? Was it by convincing my father that his view of control was barbaric, suppressive, and out of touch with democracy? No.

Mrs. Morgan leveraged my father's value! Mrs. Morgan promised to write a note every single day to my father, telling him that she had escorted my sister from practice to the bus, leaving no room for shenanigans. And she did. Mrs. Morgan wrote my father for three years. Mehret was on the team! Mehret went on to cheer during college and compete at Disney World.

When you interact with your students and families, use the lens of Values Diversity. You have your own set of values as an educator, and your families, theirs. Ask question such as, "Could you help me understand why you are pulling your student out of school for two weeks?" When you understand your students' and parents' values, you will often find that you want the same thing, such as keeping children protected and safe.

By pressing her Turbo Button, Mrs. Morgan changed the entire trajectory of my sister's high school and college experience. Mrs. Morgan remains a dear friend of my family, and this last year, came over for Thanksgiving at my sister's house.

Circles of Familiarity

WHAT KIND OF PERSON DO you connect with most easily? Who are you most likely to understand? What kind of student has a similar narrative to you, such that you automatically "get" them?

For example, I find it very easy to connect to African immigrants, particularly from countries such as Nigeria, Ghana, and of course, my homelands of Ethiopia and Eritrea. Why? In addition to our shared immigrant story, I met many of these Africans growing up and at Harvard.

As soon as I meet someone from Nigeria, I already know many things such as: there are 3 main ethnic groups in Nigeria; Nigerians value education - they have the highest PhD per capita in the world; like Ethiopians, most Nigerians got spanked by their parents.

How about you? Who do you connect with most easily? Consider the **Circles of Familiarity**:

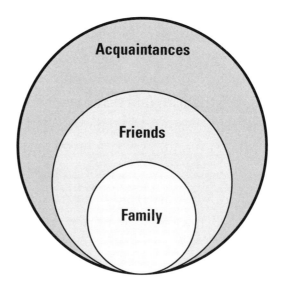

Family: Which students are like family to you? You instinctively get them. Your own family dinners are like theirs. You share several passions. You've connected with many students like them.

Friends: Which students are you comfortable with - you can connect with a little effort. You have at least one thing in common. You've interacted with students like them before.

Acquaintances: All you really know about these students is that they are at your school.

Some of the key factors that shape your Circles of Familiarity include: religion, race, political beliefs, hobbies, and places you've lived.

My Circle might look like this:

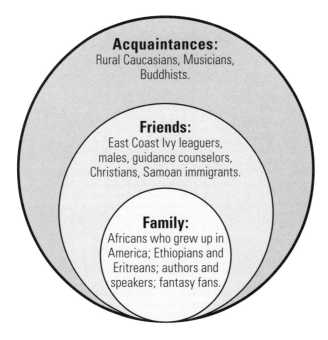

Acquaintances: Rural Caucasians, Musicians, Buddhists.

Friends: East Coast Ivy leaguers, males, guidance counselors, Christians, Samoan immigrants.

Family: Africans who grew up in America; Ethiopians and Eritreans; authors and speakers; fantasy fans.

Another way to think about your Circles is to consider how different students show up in your classroom:

Circle	Classroom Connection
Acquaintance	You rarely interact with this student in class. You know little of their interests or life outside of class.
Friend	You call on this student in class once a week. You occasionally talk with them outside of class.
Family	You banter with this student before or after class. You know their interests outside of school.

How to Use the Circles of Familiarity

THE CIRCLES OF FAMILIARITY ARE a tool to help you reflect on your own connections and the connections that come most naturally to your staff.

None of us can press an easy button and make our Acquaintance as familiar as Family - that's not the point. Nor is it helpful to beat ourselves up for not knowing enough about a certain type of student.

Here are some ways to use your Circles of Familiarity:

- Create your own Circles. Develop awareness of your circles, so you know which kinds of students you connect with most easily, and which connections require something extra from you. Work with your colleagues to ensure every student in the school has at least one adult in their Friends and Family Circle.

- A school in Minnesota went from having no Somali students to over 800 in a span of five years. When your school experiences rapid demographic shifts, your staff cannot suddenly be "Family" with the new groups. But with focused training and a desire to learn, you can get your staff to a "Friend" level of familiarity.
- In all cases, remember Dale Carnegie's lesson: Be genuine. These Circles are not destiny - just a lens to help you connect.

Do Not Take it Personally

DURING MY FRESHMAN YEAR AT Harvard, I took the bus every Tuesday afternoon to a low-income neighborhood in Boston. Along with thirty of my classmates, I would tutor kids and help them with their homework.

I was assigned to an African-American fifth-grader named Lucy. After trying to make some small talk, I'd ask her to pull out her homework. Sometimes I had to ask her five or six times just to get her assignment out. When we started the assignment, she'd stare right past me.

I looked around the room - everyone else seemed to be working well with their tutors. Lucy, I came to realize, simply did not like working with me. This surprised me - like Lucy, I was a black student who had grown up in low-income housing. On the surface at least, I had more in common with Lucy than most Harvard students did.

After the seventh week, I wondered: Why am I doing this? Clearly Lucy is not benefiting, and if I'm having no impact, I'd rather save my bus money and play basketball after class.

I talked to my coordinator and his answer surprised me. I thought he was going to say, "Keep trying." Instead, he said, "We sometimes find that some students are more comfortable with certain adults." The next week, I was assigned to a student named Marcus. Marcus and I hit it off from the first day. I tutored him the whole year.

What happened? I was being as genuine as I knew how and trying my best to connect.

In some situations, for no fault of our own, each of us will find it hard to connect with a particular student. Chemistry does matter.

It is unreasonable to expect that you will connect with every single student at a high level. Make a strong effort, and if it is not working, ask a different educator or volunteer to work with a student. Get to know another student where there might be a stronger fit.

Lucy, for example, got a new tutor. And it worked out well for everyone. As I tutored Marcus, I would look over and see Lucy smiling and talking.

Relationship Structure

A PRINCIPAL NAMED STEVE HAMLIN harnessed the power of relationships to drive student achievement. Steve's school had sixty Hispanic students that came from predominantly low-income backgrounds and had lower attendance and grades than their white counterparts.

Steve selected Horace, a teacher who had demonstrated an ability to connect with students and gave Horace training on how to talk with students in a one-on-one setting. Steve gave Horace time off during the school's three lunch periods. Each period, Horace had lunch with two Hispanic students, for a total of thirty students per week. Thus, the sixty Hispanic students each had lunch with Horace every two weeks.

During those lunches, Horace came to know each student; he also helped them set and track goals. Just the process of learning his student's academic and personal goals put the students in Horace's Friend circle.

Grades, test scores, and attendance skyrocketed for the sixty students - attendance alone rose from 75% to 95%.

Here's the point: Steve could have just asked his staff to develop relationships. Instead, he allocated specific time and created a structure that built positive relationships.

Think about your school, and the countless demands you have to increase student achievement and meet standards. What kind of structures can you create that automatically nurture relationships? How might you connect with your school's Acquaintances?

Procedural Justice

WHAT HAPPENS WHEN YOU FIND a young person doing something wrong? Or when you find them in the wrong place, such as the hallway when they should be in class?

I posed this question recently to the police chief of a major city, and he shared the following with me. When his officers enter a new situation, they are trained to do these two things in order:

1. Secure the situation: Statistical analyses has shown that police officers get killed more often when they do not immediately secure the situation. That means checking for guns and any other threats in an environment.

2. Educate: Instead of saying, "Listen punk, if I see you here on this corner again, I'm going to lock you up," the officers are trained to be a resource to the citizen. To say something like, "Listen, I'm stopping you because this exact corner has been the scene of several homicides in the past year. There was a gang shooting near here today and I don't want you to be caught in any crossfire."

The police chief called the second point "Procedural Justice." It's not just what we do, but how we do it. Not just what we say, but how we say it.

If a teacher sees a student in the wrong place at school, that teacher can say "You are breaking the rules. I'm taking you right to the principal's office." or "Can I help you get somewhere? Schools with clear hallways are much safer - and I want to ensure you're okay."

Having strong procedural justice goes a long way with minority students and parents, in particular. It's hard to have small things escalate when people proceed with a desire to help.

Warning Signs

YOUR SON WHO IS A sophomore in college starts calling you a little more often. He mentions that one of his classes is a bit strange and his roommate is not around much. He invites you to come visit him sometime in the spring.

You think, "Wow, that's a little strange - Tommy is usually pretty independent." You start planning the spring trip.

STOP! Do not wait until the spring. Go visit him now, in the fall.

Two, three, four seemingly innocent things strung together are not a coincidence. They are warning signs, telling you that something is amiss.

Listen to that voice in your head - you know the one that I'm talking about it. It's the voice that we've all ignored to our great detriment. The voice will tell you - "There is something wrong with Tommy." But we are so busy, or we want to so badly believe that nothing is wrong, that we ignore the voice.

And then we find out years later that our son was severely depressed throughout his sophomore year and contemplated taking his own life. We find out that our daughter suffered a severe eating disorder. We discover that our child was addicted to drugs or had joined a cult.

If you can only remember one thing in this book, please remember this: You are much smarter than you know. *You have a sixth sense that will usually tell you when something is wrong, but the sixth sense will not yell - so you have to keep your ears open.*

Educators can also see these warning signs. Sometimes kids will get sick and skip several days, even though they seem fine. Turns out someone is bullying them. Sometimes a good student will miss a whole rash of assignments and fail a quiz. Turns out their family just lost their home.

Sometimes, kids will forge their physical for their sports team, as I did. I got kicked off my 8th grade basketball team for it. I didn't know how to tell my coach that I had forged my physical because I couldn't afford it.

To adults, it's simple. Tell the school someone is bullying you. Let the teacher know you lost your home. Ask the school to help you get the physical. But to our youth, asking for help is often hard. So we have to look for warning signs and clues.

Become a Legend

GROWING UP, MY FAMILY LIVED month-to-month, so we rarely went out to eat. One of the rare times was when Burger King dropped the price of its Whopper to under a dollar. Then my dad would give my brother and me $20 and we'd zoom down the street to buy 20 whoppers. No joke. We'd put the uneaten Whoppers in the fridge and eat them for a few days.[3] We'd have this Whopper feast several times a year, but other than that, we did not eat out.

When I was in third grade, a woman named Jackie Cunningham volunteered with my mom. Every Thursday night, Jackie would show up with her wood-paneled station wagon and take my mom and my siblings and me to the local library. After tutoring my mother at the library, JACKIE WOULD TAKE US OUT TO DAIRY QUEEN.

That's how Jackie became a legend to my siblings and me. She didn't have to buy us a new house. She didn't have to buy my family a new car. All she had to do was take us to get some nachos or an ice cream cone. *And we still talk about her 25 years later!*

The point is not that you should take a child out for fast food to win their heart. The point is that it often does not take much, by adult estimation anyway, to become a legend to a young person.

Isn't that true in your life? Take a second and reflect on your own childhood. I bet you can think of one adult who you still remember fondly, and all they did was the equivalent of taking you to Dairy Queen.

They showed you through simple actions that they cared about you. And you can do the same for the youth in your life.

Buy a kid an ice cream cone. Ask them about their favorite action figure or video game. Get them a second scoop if they want. Become a legend.

---

3. Admittedly, this is a rather gross story. But those Whoppers tasted awesome.

More than Fantasy

HARRY POTTER'S STORY IS MORE than fantasy; our connection to our kids does buffer and inspire them.

And this love's power is everywhere in our culture - not just in Harry Potter, but in many of the great stories we tell. Luke Skywalker saves the galaxy in Star Wars not because he wins a light sabre battle, but because he appeals to the love that his father, Darth Vader, still has for him.

In the Bible, one of the most beloved passages by Christians around the world is written by St. Paul, writing from prison - Romans 8:38-39:

> *"For I am convinced that neither death nor life, neither angels nor demons,neither the present nor the future, nor any powers, neither height nor depth, nor anything else in all creation, **will be able to separate us** from the love of God."*

Your love for kids has a mystical, unpredictable, and vast power. Not just for the "good kids," or the kids that feel like Family. But for all your kids.

As a Powerful Educator, you exercise tremendous power simply by connecting with and loving your students.

Power Time

1. Think back to your own childhood. Who made the biggest impact on your life? What does this person mean to you?

2. Draw out your own Circles of Familiarity. Compare your Circles with a friend or colleague.

3. Is there one student you can think of right now who needs a connection with an adult? Can you provide that connection this year?

4. How are you with Procedural Justice at your school or home? Does how you talk to students prevent what you say from having full impact?

5. What structures can you put in place as a parent or educator to build relationships in a consistent manner?

POWERFUL EDUCATOR™

─────────POWER BREAK

NOW THAT YOU'VE SEEN POWERS 1 and 2, we can explore the relationship between all 5 Powers. Understanding how the Powers relate to each other will help you get the most from the rest of this book.

Turbo + Leverage

CONSIDER THIS IMAGE OF A lever. It shows that life gives all of us Impact Opportunities, where we can improve our families, our schools, and our communities. To realize these opportunities, we have to exert some energy - we have to hit our Turbo Buttons.

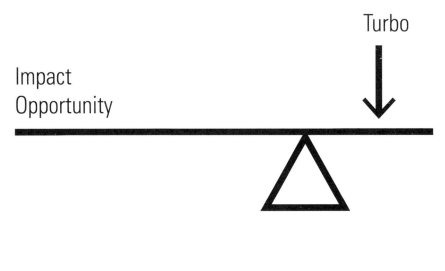

The ancient Greek, Archimedes, said, "Give me a lever long enough and I can move the world."

Relationships increase leverage. Relationships move the fulcrum so the same amount of Turbo supports much greater impact.

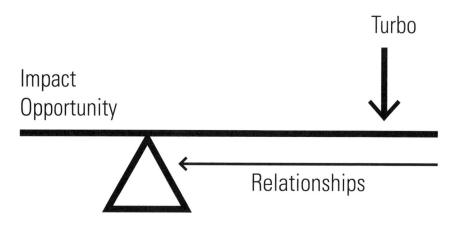

Powers 1 and 2 give you the Turbo to initiate impact and the relationships to leverage your Turbo. *Use your first two powers, and as Archimedes said, you might just move the world.*

Powers 3-5

POWERS 3-5 OFFER YOU A diagnostic and developmental framework to help you direct your Turbo. To understand Powers 3-5, consider this question: Why does a kid struggle in math?

Unless there are extenuating circumstances, it's because:

- **Power 3:** He does not *think he can* do well in math. (Mindset)
- **Power 4:** He does not *know how to* do well in math. (Skill)
- **Power 5:** He does not *want to* do well in math. (Voice)

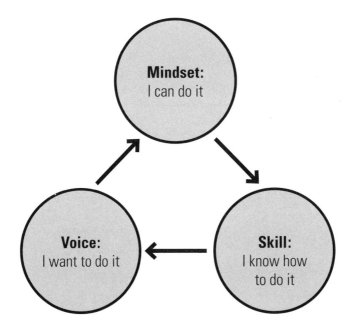

You can use Powers 3-5 as a simple diagnostic and development tool. If you see that a kid wants to learn math, but just needs extra tutoring, you focus on Power 4: Push for Skill. If you see that a kid does not care about school or math, extra tutoring sessions will not move the needle much. Build his Voice by using Power 5.

Once you finish this book, come back to this Power Break. You will see more clearly how you can use Powers 3-5 as a targeted development tool.

Why do Powerful Educators Matter?
Because our youth desperately need them.

How does someone become a Powerful Educator?
By hitting their Turbo Button and building relationships. (Powers 1 and 2)

What does someone do as a Powerful Educator?
Build Mindsets, Skill, and Voice. (Powers 3-5)

POWER 3
Speak Success Mindsets

I MET ERNESTO FOUR YEARS ago. A senior at an inner city high school, Ernesto dreamed of being the first person in his family to graduate from college. Things looked promising: Ernesto had a 35 (36 possible) on his ACT and was the president of his student body.

But there was one massive problem. Ernesto was undocumented. Even if Ernesto was accepted to a college, he would be ineligible for financial aid. In October of his senior year, Ernesto's worst fears were confirmed. Due to his documentation status, Ernesto was rejected from a scholarship program that would have paid his tuition all four years.

As Ernesto anguished over his rejection that October, he could not have known that his dreams were about to come true in spectacular fashion. But first, Ernesto would need to make one key mindset shift.

Mindsets are consistent patterns of thoughts that run on autopilot in our heads - our beliefs, our values, our vision of what's possible, our definitions of success and failure.

As adults, we have our own mindsets. Consciously or not, we speak our mindsets to our youth and thereby shape theirs. ***Speak your mindsets with care, for your words carry power beyond imagining.***

One Mindset to Rule Them All

IN THE BESTSELLING BOOK SERIES, *The Lord of the Rings,* the storyline forms around "rings of power" that give their bearers special power. As the story goes, there is one ring - THE ring of power - that rules over and controls all other rings. To save the world, the heroes must destroy this evil ring.

In her much-heralded book, *Mindsets,* Dr. Carol Dweck tells a similar story. A noted researcher from Stanford University, Dweck won the lifetime achievement award in 2013 from The American Psychological Association for her decades of research on mindsets.

While Dweck acknowledges that many mindsets contribute to success, she argues that one mindset, The Growth Mindset, is the foundational mindset that drives success. Its opposite, The Fixed Mindset, is like the evil Ring of Power. **The Fixed Mindset must be destroyed to liberate our youth and give them the highest chance of both success and happiness.**

I Guess I'm Not That Smart

I DIDN'T KNOW IT WHEN it happened, but I had a pivotal encounter with The Fixed Mindset when I was 19, during my freshman year at Harvard. I was in my first semester and taking a multivariable Calculus class.

Our entire grade would consist of three exams: 10% from the first midterm; 10% from the second mid-term; and 80% from the final. You were expected to do your homework, but your entire grade would come from exams. And the exams were curved.

I did all my homework and studied hard for my first mid-term. Disappointment mixed with fear hit me when I got my midterm back: it was a 78% on the curve, so a C+.

For my next mid-term, I studied even harder. And I got another C+.

Thoughts like the following flooded my mind:

"I guess I'm not that smart;"
"It was foolish of me to even think I could do as well as other Harvard students. These are the smartest people in the world, and I'm not one of them."
"I am public school smart, but not Harvard smart."

Dweck defines The Fixed Mindset as the belief that intelligence is fixed. Some people are born smart and others are not. Some are good at math, others are not. There is nothing anyone can do about it - it's just how the world works.

In my math class at Harvard, I felt that I had met my intelligence threshold. I was trying hard but I lacked the intelligence to score above a C.

Study What You Don't Know

When I was in seventh grade, my English teacher, Mrs. Countryman, said something simple that I never forgot.

She told our class: "The best way to study for a test is to study what you don't know. What's the point of endlessly reviewing what you already know?"

While it might make us feel more comfortable to get practice problems right, what really helps us is when we get them wrong, and then figure out why.

Dr. Dweck would call Mrs. Countryman's philosophy The Growth Mindset. The Growth Mindset is the belief that intelligence can be developed through effort. Our brains, like any muscle, get stronger through practice. But only if we are willing to get things wrong. Only if we embrace failure. Only if we study what we don't know.

My freshman year at Harvard, I was at a mindset fork in the road: I could choose to believe that my math intelligence was fixed; or I could believe that I could grow it through effort.

Harvard gives its students a generous "Reading Period" before our finals, ten days without any classes where we can focus 100% on preparing. During that time, I did more practice problems than I had done the entire semester. I do not exaggerate when I say I completed over 100 pages of problems, and every single time, I looked to understand why I got a problem wrong.

I got a 94% on the Calculus final. More importantly, The Growth Mindset solidified even further in my mind. ***Being a Harvard student did not make me intelligent - my level of effort did.***

The Can Do and Not Yet Circle

IN OUR STUDENT LEADERSHIP CLASSES, we teach students about the Can Do Circle and the Not Yet Circle.

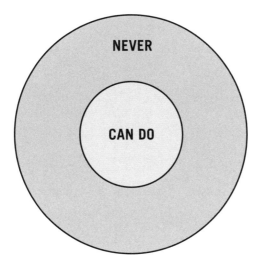

The Can Do Circle represents all the things you can do. For example, reading or driving a car.

The Not Yet Circle represents all the things you cannot do yet. For example, operating a crane is likely in your Not Yet Circle.

The following story about high school track shows why these two circles matter.

When I was a high school freshman, I ran on the track team and could complete the mile in 4 minutes and 50 seconds. I set a goal to break the school record of 4:18 by my senior year.

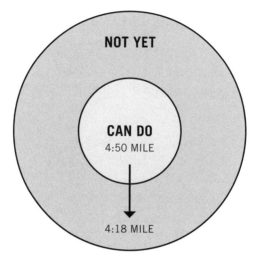

I ran track for four years and did everything in my power to break the record. I ran with icicles along my face during some brutal Chicago winter days. I even changed my diet dramatically - refusing to drink any soda my last two years of high school because I thought it would slow me down.

Despite my best effort, I failed. I did not reach my goal of 4:18 seconds.

What is Failure?

THE CAN DO AND NOT YET CIRCLES can help us adopt powerful mindsets about what success and failure look like in our lives.

I failed to run the 4:18. But I did run a mile in 4:28 at the County Championships my senior year.

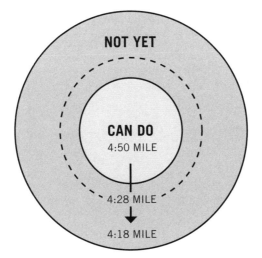

While I did not reach my goal of 4:18, my Can Do Circle had expanded dramatically to include a 4:28 mile.

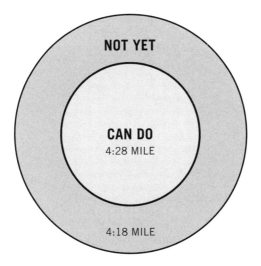

And that's what Success and Failure really look like.

Success: Taking action to grow your Can Do Circle.

Failure: Doing nothing to expand your Can Do Circle.

Just by putting forth effort, I had succeeded. Later in my Calculus class at Harvard, I succeeded not because I got a 94, but because I took the effort to grow.

The Fixed Mindset Trap

IN HER WRITINGS AND RESEARCH, Dweck shows how the Fixed Mindset devastates students of all backgrounds.

Take for example, Sarah, a high school junior from Jacksonville. From a young age, Sarah was told by her teachers and parents that she was a gifted student. She was born blessed with innate intelligence.

Each year, Sarah felt more and more pressure to validate just how smart she was. Every class, every test, every homework assignment was a referendum on her intelligence.

By the time Sarah got to her junior year, her life felt like a pie-eating contest - the more A's Sarah "ate," the more A's she had to eat! She had to get into the top colleges. She had to excel at that top college and land a top job. She'd have to have the best performance reviews at her top job someday.

More than her intelligence was at stake - her basic self-worth and value as a human being was connected to a definition of success that left no room for error.

Students with the Fixed Mindset live in perpetual fear that the world will find out that they really are not that intelligent. Their quest for perfection spews constant anxiety.

At the other end of the spectrum, John is a "D" student at his high school. John figured out long ago that he could never compete with students like Sarah. Sarah was one of those kids who was "just born smart." So John put forth enough effort to keep his parents off his back and to graduate, but he never challenged himself. What was the point of trying when it would just lead to the pain of failure?

Dweck calls students like John "low effort syndrome students." These students conclude it's better to give up than to risk probable failure or to have to work hard.

Too Scared To Try

LET'S GO BACK TO ERNESTO, the undocumented high school senior who dreamt of going to college. After he was rejected by the scholarship he had counted on, Ernesto's entire demeanor changed. He had failed. And the sting of rejection hurt.

He wondered if he should get a job working as a mechanic like his father.

Most people don't know that the most expensive schools, like Harvard, are often the most generous schools. For example, today, any student whose family makes less than $60,000 gets an automatic full-ride scholarship to Harvard.

Of course, one has to get accepted by Harvard first. When I asked Ernesto to apply, he looked at me like I had grown five heads. I was expecting this response. So I told him that I had called a good friend who works in the admissions office at Harvard and asked her if they would consider an undocumented student. She said they would.

In Ernesto's eyes, I could see that he would not apply. He was too scared that he would be rejected again. And deep down he did not believe he could be a Harvard student.

I Can Do It

WHEN YOU SAY, "I can do it," what do you risk? That you will fall flat on your face. That people will know that you "failed." That you will have to carry that "failure" for the rest of your life.

Failure is too high a price for people trapped in the Fixed Mindset - they'd rather stay in the comfort of their Can Do Circle. They would rather work as a mechanic with no chance of failure, than risk being rejected by Harvard.

And that's where Power 2: Relate with Heart comes in. Ernesto had developed tremendous trust with his principal, his guidance counselor, and other educators at his school. Together we told him again, and again, that he needed to apply. Here is an excerpt from a letter he wrote me:

"You mentioned how I had created this opportunity for myself, how my hard work had set me up to have this chance at Harvard. *After some reflection, I learned to believe you.*"

Ernesto did not believe me the first or second time. And your students may not believe you right away either. That's why we have to speak Success Mindsets again and again.

Today, Ernesto is an undergraduate student at Harvard and Harvard has paid virtually the entire cost of his education. One of my favorite moments in life was visiting him during his freshmen year.

That's the power of mindset. A student can go from "I'm undocumented and cannot go to college" to "I am at Harvard."

Powerful Mindsets

HERE ARE SOME OF THE mindsets that Powerful Adults instill in students:

I can grow my abilities with effort.

I succeed anytime I take action to grow.

Anyone of any race and background can succeed through hard work.

I am great anytime I serve.

Challenges can fuel unexpected growth and opportunity.

I cannot fail. I can only learn and grow.

When I forgive others, bitterness and hatred lose their power over me.

I am at my greatest when I remember those who are most vulnerable in my community.

If you had to pick three mindsets that you want to instill in youth, what would they be? Go ahead and write them out and post them somewhere in your classroom or home. I'll buy you a sandwich.

Refugee Mindset

Over the years, I've been lucky enough to know many refugees. Many of them are from Ethiopia and Eritrea, but others are from Somalia, Burma, Kosovo - really, all over the globe.

Refugees have one mindset that has always amazed and inspired me. HOPE. Despite their suffering and challenges, refugees have hope. They do not view their challenges as a death knell, but rather they expect challenges as a natural part of life, and do their best.

In the U.S., we often expect the opposite. We expect things to work out and when they do not, we feel ripped off. We feel unlucky. I do this too, even though I used to live in a hut in a refugee camp. *I get mad when the power goes out in Chicago, even though I lived for years without any power in Sudan.*

Sometimes, when I'm stuck at an airport with endless delays, I wonder: How in the world can this airline mess it up again? But then I tell myself: *There was a time when you never thought you'd be on an airplane. For most of human history, people had to spend five months walking or riding a horse to do what we now do in three or four hours. So it's okay to have a delay.* When I make this mindset shift, my stress level goes down. I pull out my computer and start playing video games.

Schools are complex organizations. A million different things can go wrong on any given day. Parents: Give your administrators and teachers grace. Educators, give yourself some grace.

The expectation cannot be that everything has to go right all the time or a school is doing poorly. In fact, the only sane explanation for parents and schools is: *Things will go wrong. Every day. And that's okay. That's what it means to be a parent or educator.*

We get up, day after day, and we do our best. We remember that challenges simply mean we are alive.

Speak the Mindset

As a Powerful Educator, challenge yourself to intentionally speak Success Mindsets. For example:

- When a student performs well, say "You showed great effort" (Growth) instead of "You are so smart," (Fixed).
- When your child spills some milk, ask them, "What do we do when we spill in our family?" After a second, speak your Success Mindset: "We clean it up." *We don't waste time in our family blaming people or screaming - we just fix things and move on.* Of course, your child can lead in the cleanup.
- When a student struggles with a concept, you can say: "We get smarter by getting things wrong, and then figuring out why."
- When a student sets a goal and does not reach it, you can say: "Success is anytime you take action to grow."

How about negative mindsets? In many homes and staff lounges, one can hear negative mindsets such as, "*That* group of kids can't achieve."

Even if you never say these negative mindsets to a kid, the mindsets have tremendous power. How? Because you can actually feel a school's mindsets within two minutes of being there.

Try it next time you enter a building. You will feel the mindset, the culture, the beliefs of the adults in a building. Parents can feel it. Students can feel it.

That's why test prep interventions and "Achievement Gap" programs have limited impact at many schools. Mindsets exert an unavoidable gravitation pull on our conversations and actions 24/7.

And to be clear, mindsets come from us, from adults. When we blame students for their mindsets, we give up access to our Turbo Button and deny ownership of our own power.

Your Kids are Listening!

As a history major, I've always loved those spectacular moments when people publicly declare their minds. Dr. King speaking out his dream. Our Founding Fathers declaring a new form of government. Going back to 1517, Martin Luther pounding his 95 Theses onto a church door.

These leaders sparked massive change because they actively spoke their mindsets. You are the same way. You have power when you speak your Success Mindsets. When you post them in your home. When you post them in your classroom. When you remind your students and kids again and again.

When I speak to high schools, students often come up to me and say, "My mom and dad have been telling me the same thing my whole life." **See, your kids are listening!** Kids won't always let you know that they are listening, especially as they get older and put on their "cool hats." But they hear you more often than you know.

Think about your own journey. How many times did your

parents tell you certain things before you got them? In the introduction to this book, I told you that I shoplifted during middle school, even though my parents and church had taught me for years not to steal.

Educators, how about the student who seems like she will never come around? Give her the same Success Mindset you give the compliant learner who "gets it" the first time. Maybe she has heard negative mindsets her whole life - maybe you are the first person to ever speak these mindsets to her.

Students believe on their own timeline, not ours.

Like a Sun Blazing!

Have you ever caught an accidental glimpse of the noonday sun, at the height of its glory in full summer? Did the brightness not stun you and overwhelm you before you looked away?

That's how I feel when I see an educator or parent in the full glory of their power, when they are hitting their Turbo Button, relating to kids, and speaking Success Mindsets. These powerful, magnificent adults bring stunning hope and opportunity to kids.

These Powerful Educators do it in quiet moments, when a child is about to give up: "Listen. I know this is hard. But remember what we always talk about: it's supposed to be hard. We get strong by doing hard things. And I believe in you!"

They do it when kids are just starting school, as my parents did for me when I was six. My dad told me, "Someday you are going to get a scholarship to college." I lived on food stamps; I didn't know any English; I didn't know anything about the United States; but I knew one thing: I could get a scholarship to college!

By this point in the book, you know who that noonday sun is. It's not someone else, some other powerful educator or parent. It's YOU. It's who you are meant to be for our youth. Even when you are tired. Even when you feel overwhelmed. Even when you feel like you do not know what you are doing.

You are that noonday sun. And you are only going to get brighter as we unlock your Fourth and Fifth powers.

Power Time

1. What Success Mindsets helped you in your own journey as a student?
2. For your home or school, what are the top three Success Mindsets you want to speak?
3. What is the Mindset gravitational pull like at your school or home? What do people "feel" as soon as they enter? What would you like them to feel?
4. If there was one Mindset shift you needed to make personally, what would it be?

POWERFUL EDUCATOR™

POWER 4
Push for Skill

SWEAT DRENCHED MY BACK. THE rhythmic pounding of running shoes mixed with the steady chatter of track-and-field athletes.

My mile race would start in less than five minutes. And the competition terrified me. Two of the runners had made all-conference the previous year. On the wet grass, next to the track, I kneeled on one knee and asked God for strength and stamina.

When the starter's gun went off, I quickly tucked in behind the two lead runners and vowed to stick with them to the end. In the mile, the pack often separates in the third lap, as the more aggressive and skilled runners go for the jugular, hoping to build an insurmountable lead before the fourth and final lap.

As we started the third lap, the lead runners kicked things up a gear. I followed for half a lap. Then, gasping for air, my legs wobbling, I helplessly saw them pull away.

I learned an important lesson my first season of high school track. Prayer is great. Having a positive mindset is great. But at some point you need to be able to run. You need skill.

Powerful educators and parents go beyond relationships and mindsets to build skill in their students.

Kiss Your Teacher's Feet

WHEN I SPEAK TO HIGH school students, I often ask how many like it when their teachers assign long papers. Groans erupt. A few scattered hands go up.

I then say, "If your teacher assigns a five-page paper, you should immediately kiss that teacher's feet." As you can expect, students do not agree.

I explain to students that colleges and employers both identify writing as the skill most lacking in students. And there is only one way to really improve at writing. Feedback. You write your crummy or average sentence. Someone who knows more than you tells you how to fix it.

For example, I had an editor who helped me see that strong writers avoid filler phrases like "in order." Consider this sentence "He went to his boss in order to ask for a raise." Now compare to this tighter sentence: "He went to his boss to ask for a raise." I never would have known to cut phrases like "in order" without the help of this editor.

I can remember that at my high school, each English teacher had about 150 students. *So if that teacher assigned a 5-page paper, he or she had to grade 750 pages.* Anyone who has graded papers knows 750 pages, read closely, take at least 20 hours of work. And our English teachers are already busy: They teach all day; they plan their lessons; and they have families of their own. So they have to give up entire weekends to grade one assignment.

When that teacher assigns you that five-page paper, and grades it closely, they are giving you a piece of their life. They don't have to teach you to delete "in order" - they can choose to scrawl 95% on top with a "Nice Job."

Powerful Educators make great personal sacrifices to build skill in students. They take time to see where a student is and make specific recommendations to move that student forward. That's why we should kiss these educators' feet.

Powerful Parents do the same thing. The mother, who after a long and exhausting day, takes five minutes to coach her son on his violin. The father who helps his daughter with her homework, even though he has tremendous pressure at work. The aunt or uncle who makes financial sacrifice to enroll their nephew in a swimming program.

Skill comes from hard work and a feedback loop that builds mastery. And there are simply no shortcuts.

The Science Behind Skill

NO RESEARCHER HAS DONE MORE to highlight the importance of skill than Dr. Martin Seligman. Dr. Seligman is the past chair of the American Psychological Association and the current chair of the Psychology Department at the University of Pennsylvania.

For decades, Dr. Seligman focused his research on one question: *How can adults help students develop confidence?*

After studying over 100,000 students, Dr. Seligman found that the self-esteem movement of the late 20th century had actually hurt many kids. In his landmark book, *The Optimistic Child*, Dr. Seligman shows that the best way to build confidence is not to tell kids that they are great, but to help them develop real skills.

Confidence is not a stairway that we build for students and ask them to climb. Confidence is a stairway that students must construct for themselves one skill at a time.

When We Fail Students

I GET INVITED OFTEN BY inner city schools to give messages about the importance of dreaming. Early in my career, I would happily give these speeches. The more I studied the research of Dr. Seligman and others, the more I realized that theses speeches alone could not help students.

Too much dreaming and not enough skill sets students up for a rude awakening. Students get into college, but they drop out because they are years behind in math and reading. Or they don't get into college because they got a 14 (36 possible) on their ACT.

One of my most depressing experiences in education came when I met a student named Rico at an inner city school in Washington State. After I spoke to his school, I met with Rico because he wanted to attend an Ivy League school. The principal and guidance counselor told me Rico was an incredible student; straight A's; he was the pride of the school.

I sat with Rico to get the basics of his application. GPA: 4.0/4.0. Student Body President. Then came the test scores. 17 out of 36 on his ACT. 820 out of 1600 on his SAT.

My friends tell me that I rarely get mad. But that day, I made a call to the superintendent and asked why the district was shortchanging

Rico. For a kid like Rico, testing anxiety was not the issue, nor was it Rico's level of effort.

The school had failed Rico, plain and simple. His classes were too easy. He was not challenged nearly enough. He was told he was ready for college ball, when skill-wise he couldn't make most high school teams.

Even more terrifying: If that was how the school was challenging Rico, what was happening to the rest of the students?

We fail our students not because we challenge them too much, but because we do not challenge them enough.

To Rico's superintendent's credit, he increased the rigor in the ensuing years. For example, he added Advanced Placement classes for the first time.

Math Champions

IN ILLINOIS, AN INNER-CITY HIGH school has never won the State Math Championship. Suburban powerhouses such as the Illinois Math and Science Academy have won every single year. Until last year, when a Chicago Public High School, Whitney Young, won the crown.

I read about the two Math team coaches in the *Chicago Tribune* and the *Chicago Sun-Times*. And last summer, I interviewed one of the coaches at Mawi Learning's annual Powerful Educator summer conference.[4]

Relentless practice. That was how they won. They practiced

---

4. You can learn more about the conference at PowerfulEducator.com.

like a basketball team does: every day, after school, for hours.

When I interviewed the math coach, Julienne, I could think of only one word to describe her: **Fierce**. Not because Julienne raised her voice or waved a sword around. But because she had a quiet, unwavering strength when it came to skill development.

You will practice hard on my math team. In my freshman Geometry class, I will give you the first D of your life if you are lazy - I don't care if you got an A on every math class prior to me because you could skate on talent. And if your mom calls me to ask why you got a D, I will tell her that's what you earned. You can change your grade anytime - you just have to work harder.

Powerful educators like Julienne push students because skill development is hard, hard work. Students will look you in the eye and say, "This is too hard," or "I can't do this," or "I'm sick of practicing."

Do. Not. Back. Off. Backing off may be expedient in the short term, but it inhibits long-term skill development. Look right back at them and say, "I show you I believe in you by challenging you."

Not Ever

Let's say that you are a school principal, and you are working with the math department to implement some new, more challenging standards. Here is one standard you have adopted:

CCSS.MATH.PRACTICE.MP3 Construct viable arguments and critique the reasoning of others.

To meet this standard, you have asked the math department to have students do Math Talks. A Math Talk is where students do math problems at the board, in front of all their classmates.

One of your teachers, named Henry, comes in and tells you: "Look, our kids can't do the Math Talks. It's too hard for them."

What just happened? *Instead of a Not Yet Circle, Henry has created a Not Ever Circle for the students.* Just like it sounds, the Not Ever Circle assumes students will never achieve something.

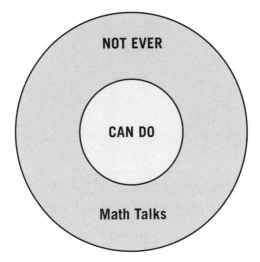

The Not Ever Circle focuses on an unattainable endpoint instead of incremental student growth. It robs you of Turbo and leads to powerless, Victim conversations.

For example, the Victim conversation between you and Henry might go something like:

- "Well, last year's teachers did a bad job so of course the students can't do Math Talks."
- "Our kids have always struggled in math so this is no surprise."
- "I told you these standards were too hard. Remember?"

Not Yet

How could you flip this Victim Conversation into a Turbo Conversation? To get started, replace the Not Ever Circle with a Not Yet Circle.

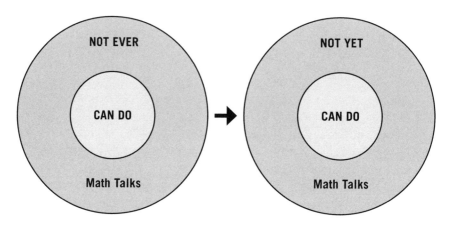

Next, ask Henry what the kids CAN DO today. In a worst case scenario, Henry might say, "They can watch me do Math."

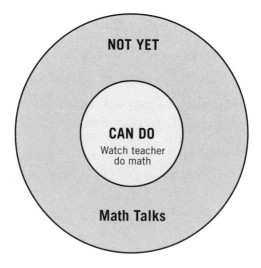

Now you are ready to ask a Turbo Question that stimulates growth. A Turbo Question starts with: "What can we do this week to grow the Can Do Circle?"

In this case, "What can we do this week to help students grow their Can Do so they get closer to doing Math Talks?" You and Henry might decide:

- We will have the students do Math Talks with problems they already can do, so students get used to standing at the board.
- We will have students do Math Talks in pairs at their desk instead of at the board.
- We will train students on how to give feedback to classmates.

Compare this Turbo Conversation to the Victim Conversation earlier. Which conversation will stimulate growth? Which conversation do you want to have at your school this coming year?

To have consistent Turbo Conversations that promote growth:

1. **Use the Right Circle:** Use Not Yet instead of Not Ever.
2. **Identify Can Do:** Focus on what students can already do, not what they will never do.
3. **Ask a Turbo Question:** What can we do this week to increase Can Do?

To Run Faster, Run Faster

POWERFUL EDUCATORS PUSH FOR SKILL not just in math and literacy, but in bedrock non-cognitive skills such as goal-setting, time management, and grit.

But how do we do it? Say you are a Superintendent of a 100,000 student system. Say you are a parent of a 5th grader. Say you lead a class of 12 Special Education students. How do you develop real skill in the "life skills?"

Last year my wife ran four marathons, and if I may brag for a moment, she did well enough to qualify for the Boston Marathon. When some of her friends asked her how to run faster, Erin gave this scientific advice, "To run faster, run faster." Turn up the speed on the treadmill. Go a little harder on your next practice run. Just do it.

Consider the following diagram that highlights the 70-20-10 rule, used by corporations worldwide to train their staff. It shows that 10% of learning comes from listening; 20% from discussing; and 70% from experience.

The 70–20–10 Rule

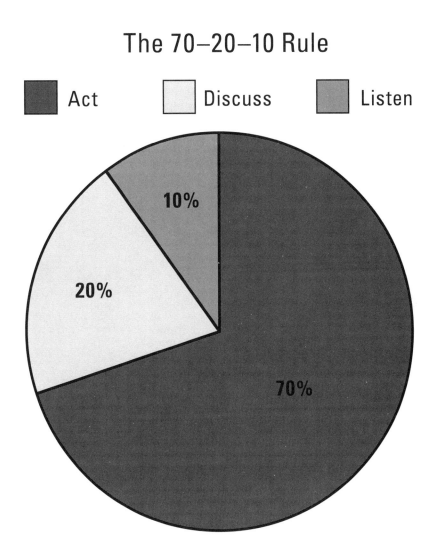

Dr. Seligman's life research with students makes the same point. Nothing substitutes for the students having mastery in their own life. Doing is the best way to learn.

The Action Wheel™

HERE IS A SIMPLE TOOL that I have used with educators and students across North America. It's called The Action Wheel, and it gives any educator or parent a simple way to "Run Faster" when it comes to character building.

1. Explore: Pick a character quality or skill and explain it to a student. Do not stop exploring until the student can explain the quality on their own.
2. Plan: Help the student make a plan of how they will use that quality in their own life in the coming week.
3. Act: Track with the student as they implement the character quality.
4. Reflect: Debrief with the student, along with the other students.

If you are looking for character qualities to explore, start with what CASEL.org offers for free on their website. CASEL stands for the Collaborative on Social and Emotional Learning and is widely regarded as a leading think tank for character education.

CASEL's research shows that the following five skills matter most: self-awareness, self-management, social awareness, relationship skills, and responsible decision making.

Maybe you disagree with CASEL's model. Maybe you think that relationship skills are too close to social awareness, and that at your school, you need to focus more on conflict resolution.

No problem. You can tailor your list of character qualities to your own school as needed. What you want to avoid is staying stuck at Step 1 of the Action Wheel, Explore, where you debate character qualities endlessly.

Get your students around the Action Wheel, whether for conflict resolution or relationship skills. It's the process of gaining mastery, of DOING, that matters most. In Appendix C, I give you step-by-step instructions for getting around the Action Wheel and provide a specific example.

Why is It So Hard?

MANY OF YOU READING ABOUT the Action Wheel are undoubtedly thinking:

I'm an English teacher and I'm already so busy meeting my content standards. How will I have time to do this kind of in-depth character building?

By the time I get my three kids ready for school, go to work for 8 hours, pick my kids back up, help them with their homework, and feed them dinner, I'm EXHAUSTED!

I get it. Educators and parents are busy.

So here are some things you can do:

- **Pick Your # of Loops:** Pick the number of Action Loops that work for you. In our work with schools, we typically help schools build in 3-5 Action Loops for each student in a specific year. Maybe at your school, you will help students go through the Action Wheel process once a semester. Not being able to do everything you might want does not mean you cannot do SOMETHING.
- **Adjust the Action Time:** You can have students take action for a day, week, or month. Adjust the action time to what works best for you.
- **Focus on Turbo:** Instead of using the Action Wheel, focus on the Turbo Button. Keep asking students, how can you hit your Turbo Button this week? Anytime you teach a character principle, ask students to apply it that same day.

However you choose to do it, get your students to use their character training in specific ways in their own lives. Only by practicing in K-12, can the students show up ready to use their life skills on their college campus and their adult lives.

The Power of Routine

I HAD ONE ROUTINE IN high school that got me into Harvard. Every evening at 6:00 I started doing my homework. And I wouldn't stop until I was done. Sometimes I finished in an hour. Other times, I worked past midnight.

I didn't stop and think, "I wonder when I should do my homework today." Nor did I think, "Where should I do it?" I did it in the same place every time: in my room, on a little adjustable bench press.

The best way to build skill is not to get motivated, *but to set up structures that make motivation unnecessary.* For example, basketball practice is every day, at 3:00. No motivation is needed because it's not a choice. If you are on the team, you go every single day at the same exact time.

If you are a parent, you can train your student to do their homework at the same exact time, every day so it is not a choice.

My son knows that every single day, he practices his viola for 15 minutes. It's not a choice for us or for him. (Okay, so there is still a little bit of arguing sometimes, but far less than would be without the consistent expectation and routine.)

I train college students to create study havens for themselves. Places where no one can find them, such as a secluded section of their library deep in the stacks. Students schedule four ironclad study times in their haven each week. Each session is two hours.

By following this one success ritual each week, students drastically limit the chance they will fail out for academic reasons and set themselves up for success.

1% Better

AT THE START OF THE 1986-87 NBA basketball season, L.A. Lakers coach Pat Riley had a problem. The previous spring, his team had given everything it had, all season long - and had still fallen short of the title, defeated by their arch-enemies, the Boston Celtics.

Riley needed a new strategy. But he knew he couldn't crack the whip; all of his players had tested their limits the previous season.

So when Riley addressed the team, he asked each player a simple question: "Can you push yourself every day to be just 1% better than you were a year ago?"

Riley knew that if you ask someone to be two or three times better, their mind will rebel. They'll say it's impossible - they can't even fathom it. But 1% better? Any one of us can do that.

Once his players accepted the challenge, their performance didn't jump by 1%, it skyrocketed. Their statistical improvement was vast; their record one of the best in NBA history. By focusing on small, believable, and attainable improvements, each player grew, and the team won the championship.

Push for Skill does not mean that we make onerous demands of ourselves or our students. It means we challenge our students to grow little by little, day after day. It means that we keep pushing for incremental growth even when we see little progress. And we do it in both academic areas like math and literacy and in character development.

Consider how water boils. When it is at 140 or 160 degrees, it seems like nothing is happening. You keep the flame on, and when it gets to 212 something magical happens. Vapors rise, bubbles pop, and the boiling point is reached.

Our students are the same. Before our students wield Jedi-like, "magical" powers, they have to build their energy little by little, skill by skill. And you, Powerful Educator, are there to push them.

Power Time

1. What character skills matter most for your students? Is your school or home adequately teaching these skills?
2. What kind of time and budget resources does your school or home allocate toward character skills?
3. Do your students give you resistance when you Push for Skill? How might you overcome this resistance?
4. In your own life, go around the Action Wheel. Pick one of these three qualities: forgiveness, initiative, or service.

POWERFUL EDUCATOR™

POWER 5
Champion Voice

SEVERAL YEARS AGO, A MAGAZINE COVER article caught my eye. The article showed a teenaged girl surfing, and had the tagline, "Taylor Cottrell lives to surf. But she would tell you that she surfs to live."

I had no idea that this one article would crystallize the essence of our Fifth Power.

Taylor dreamt of being a typical teenager - going to school, hanging out with friends, developing her independence. But she suffered from a rare autoimmune illness that confined her to a wheelchair. By the time Taylor was thirteen, her illness had ravaged her body so relentlessly that she had to stay home. Her friends could not visit for fear that a bacteria or virus they carried could end Taylor's life.

Taylor saw doctor after doctor, but none could help her. And then Taylor told her mother something that would pack unexpected, transformative power: *I want to surf.*

Taylor had always dreamed of surfing. If she were going to die from her illness, she wanted to surf first. After much soul-searching, Taylor's mother relented, and Taylor went to a special surfing school run by a non-profit in California.

Doctors do not have a scientific explanation for what happened next: Taylor's illness receded and she experienced a spectacular full recovery. On the cover of Southwest's Spirit Magazine, Taylor flashed the kind of happy smile we want to see on all our youth.

Much as I'd like to give you an excuse to hit the beach, I am NOT saying that surfing has mystical powers, or that traditional medicine should be ignored.

But I am saying that as educators we can tap a mystifying, inspiring, and often-ignored power: we can tap, fan, and CHAMPION the unique voice inside each of our students.

Voice is that special sauce that makes you you and not anyone else on the planet. It's your passions, your dreams, your personality, and the things that motivate you as an individual.

The 8th Habit

By THIS POINT, YOU KNOW that I'm a fan of Dr. Stephen Covey and *The 7 Habits of Highly Effective People.* A few years back, I was excited when Dr. Covey decided that seven was not enough. He was writing a new book called *The 8th Habit.*

I knew that Dr. Covey would not add a Habit lightly - he had dedicated his entire life to the development of his 7 Habits. What was so important that it warranted a change to his leadership system?

Voice.

Voice is that yearning for greatness in each of our souls.

It's that passion for tennis, opera, a particular board game, fine dining, or surfing.

It's that thing you are willing to do at any hour because you LOVE IT.

As our schools are held more accountable for student test scores; as teachers are further evaluated based on those scores; we should not forget a simple truth: *Our students are not test scores. They are not evaluations. They will not care about standardized testing and growth as measured by adults - why would they? None of us did when we were kids.*

Our students do, however, care about their Voice. Like Taylor's mom, we can unlock spectacular, unimagined results when we respect, pay attention to, and champion that Voice.

The Most Violent Middle School in New York City

IMAGINE YOU GOT THE FOLLOWING phone call:

We need your help. JHS 22 is the most violent middle school in all of New York City. In some classes, only 5 out of 30 students show up. The school has had 7 principals in the last two years. We want you to be the 8th.

What would you do? I met Shimon, the newly appointed principal at a training I did for the Harvard School of Education.

Shimon had paid for college by serving in the R.O.T.C program with the United States Army. His service included time as an intelligence officer where he developed his skills in counter-insurgency.

As Shimon told me when I visited his school, "I knew the only way I could win was to get the students to be a part of the solution. So I recruited the students, one at a time, starting with the ones that had the most influence."

To show that he meant business, Shimon gave students real power over budgetary decisions such as what speakers visited the school and what supplementary activities the school funded. Shimon held weekly listening sessions with small groups of students.

Not everyone applauded Shimon's focus on Voice. After all, why give student budgetary power when that money could be used for new textbooks? Shimon argued that students needed more than new textbooks - they needed to feel a sense of their own power.

In less than two years, the school culture transformed - attendance skyrocketed to 93%; the school earned an A rating on student testing; the school was no longer on the list of the 12 most violent schools in New York (the others on the list were all high schools). And Shimon had outlasted his predecessors.

By enlisting students to lead the change, Shimon tapped the power of Voice and transformed the school's culture.

The Voice of The Action Wheel

VOICE IS BUILT RIGHT INTO the Action Wheel.

In the planning phase, let students choose any action they want, as long as the actions are safe. If you are studying Initiative, a student may make the following plan: "I will learn two new skateboarding tricks by the end of this week."

You may look at the student and think, "The last thing you need to work on is your skateboarding. You have an F in math right now."

But as soon as you say, "Why don't you work on math," you become just another Voice-killing adult.

Connect with your student first on his terms and he will be more likely to care about your class and school. And while he may

not build math skills in this loop of the Action Wheel, he is building his own agency and developing his goal-setting skills.

When a student knows how to set goals and follow through, they have a higher chance of succeeding in math. Indeed, many researchers point out that the divide between cognitive (math, literacy) and non-cognitive (character skills like goal-setting) is artificial, as both are necessary and together drive student learning.

Examples of Voice

So how do you do it? If you are a school, what are some simple ways you can develop Voice?

1. **Allocate Structured Time:** At Vincent Massey K-8 school, students have a weekly Options hour, where the students can pick from a number of activities, including Hip-Hop dance, drama, guitar, jewelry making, photography, movie making, and environmental issues.

2. **Organize Listening Sessions:** Meet with small groups of students from all backgrounds to ask them about their needs and concerns. I once sat with district leaders in Oregon and asked ELL students why they did not do more activities. Rides. It was that simple. The school got the students transportation, and student involvement skyrocketed.

3. **Create Marquee Events:** In Rhode Island, an educator named Laurie Beauvais organizes a March Madness basketball tournament every year. Students of

all backgrounds and abilities organize into randomly assigned teams and have their own tournament. The students look forward to it, and it has become a core part of the school culture.

4. **Service Projects:** Few things inspire students as much as authentic service opportunities, where students feel themselves making an impact. I've seen low-income schools raise 750,000 pennies for refugees; witnessed students shaving their principal's head at huge assemblies to raise money for cancer; watched kids feed the homeless.[5]

In each of these four cases, Voice is not free. You have to dedicate staff hours and in some cases, financial resources. That's why your paradigm matters. If the Testing Decade is all that you see, when push comes to shove, test prep will beat out Voice every time.

Your Voice is Yours Alone

YOU ARE NOT VINCENT MASSEY SCHOOL, or Laurie from Rhode Island. You have your own school and community. Your own students. Your own bell schedule. I cannot tell you exactly HOW to develop Voice at your school.

---

5. In Appendix D, you can find a report that synthesizes key findings from over 1,000 student service projects we helped students accomplish last year. Students led these service projects last year in the final module of Mawi Learning's Leadership Skills class.

If you want to start somewhere, start with your staff. Discuss what Voice means at your school. Do a Voice Inventory among your administrators, teachers, counselors, and support staff.

You may find, for example, that you have five staff members who are deeply passionate about writing. Maybe those five can do what the staff at Fremd High School in Illinois does. Fremd High School is renowned across Chicagoland for its Writer's Week, where authors visit for a week with students and faculty, and students develop their writing skills.

Or maybe you will find that your staff has a deep interest in international education. Maybe like Highland Middle School, those passionate staff will set up partnerships with schools in Uganda, and your students will broaden their global horizons.

Voice, whether from students or faculty, is contagious and brings its own wild positive energy. To unlock it, simply ask the question again and again, "How do we unlock Voice here at our school?"

You may hear people wonder, "If I increase Voice, will test scores rise?"

Asking if Voice increases test scores is like asking if Community Service increases test scores. It might, but that's not why you serve. And if test scores are the reason you serve, then it's no longer Community Service.

Prioritize Voice because you have a particular view of what education should be and the kind of school you want to have.

Some Men Look Better!

SOMETIMES, A COMMUNITY HAS TO take extreme measures to unlock student Voice. Consider the case of Clayton Muhammad, an educator in Aurora, IL. In 2002, Aurora saw a deadly outbreak of gang violence, largely as the result of fifteen gang leaders.

Instead of just decrying the gangs, Clayton hit his Turbo Button and asked: If the gangs could offer an exciting and alluring lifestyle, why not the schools? If the gangs could provide Voice, identity, and purpose, why not the larger community? So Clayton recruited fifteen young men and started a brotherhood called Boys 2 Men (B2M).

How you walk matters, he taught the young men. How you dress matters. How you hold your head matters. How you treat women matters. Everything matters. Clayton got B2M coverage in the local paper. He took them on college visits that showed them how exciting college life was. Clayton published a magazine and on each cover, a student wore a stunning outfit, looking much more like a model than the boring stereotype of a successful student. Consider the final stanzas from the Boys 2 Men creed:

WE KNOW
Being phenomenal is a lifestyle.
When you change your mind, you change your life.
When you know better, you do better.
All men are created equal.
Some just achieve more and look better

Some just achieve more and look better. I love the positive swagger!

Today, 100% of B2M's students go to college or serve in the military. Alumni work as professionals at Fortune 500 companies, as educators, and about 5% serve in the Armed Forces. And homicides in the city of Aurora went from 22 in 2002 to none in 2012!

But that's not all. A group of Caucasian teenagers in Australia heard about B2M and created their own B2M chapter. Picture this: *Caucasian Australian teenagers coming to Aurora, IL to learn and connect with Black and Hispanic B2M members.* If this picture of intercontinental friendship does not prove the wild, unpredictable power of Voice, I'm not sure what can.

Push for Voice

DURING HIS FRESHMAN YEAR OF high school, my brother Hntsa had a routine: Go to school, come home, do his homework, and then play video games. Hnsta was kind, respectful, and got good grades.

Still, I felt that Hntsa was missing out. I had grown throughout high school and college from playing on sports teams and other extracurricular activities. I wanted my brother to have similar opportunities to develop his Voice.

And even though I had just started my work with schools, I already saw research that showed that school involvement tracks with graduation and many other positive outcomes. You can see some of this research in Appendix B.

I asked Hntsa to join an activity at his school. *He could choose anything.* Hntsa said no.

Our father had passed away the previous year, and I didn't want to be too hard on Hntsa. At the same time, I was now the oldest male in my family, and being seven years Hntsa's senior, felt that I had to act as his father.

So I went to our mom and said, "Let me take all his video games to my apartment. Don't let him watch TV until he joins an activity."

Hntsa complained until he realized there was no way out. Then he joined the cross-country and track team. And let me tell you, it was brutal to watch his races - he never scored one point for his team, in all four years.

But Voice is not about winning or losing.

On his team, Hntsa made more than 20 new friends. He had been chubby before the team but gradually, he got in shape - he still runs today. Even though he was not on the varsity team, his classmates elected him a Co-Captain his senior year. And his coach wrote his letter of recommendation that helped him get into Duke.

As parents, we sometimes have to nudge our kids to establish their Voice. When they are younger, we have to do more of the choosing, such as piano class. But as they get older, particularly in middle and high school, let them choose, as Hntsa did.

God Did Not Make Me Like That

SOMETIMES MY WIFE DOES ART projects with my son, age five, and my daughter, who is three. They usually go at it for about 15 minutes with markers and some coloring books.

Even though my son tries hard, and has lived 40% longer than my daughter, she colors much better than he does. One day, as my wife was pushing him, he told her, "Mommy, I'm trying but God did not make me that way."

The Growth Mindset in me wanted to retort, *"NO! That is not the right way to think. We can all work hard and improve."*

But the truth is we are all made differently. Math comes more naturally to some of us; writing to others; piano to others. Some of us love to organize, others to sell, and still others to create.

As adult professionals, we accept that our colleagues each have their own competencies and wirings. *Why then do we treat all of our students the same?*

When we champion our students' Voice, we don't prevent our students from excelling in bedrock areas like literacy and math. We enliven and respect our student's humanity, and prepare them to share their Voice with the world.

Power Time

1. What is your Voice? What activity would you do at midnight?
2. How does your school currently Champion Voice? How do you do it in your home?
3. At your school, is there a particular passion area shared by many staff? How could you develop your staff's Voice?
4. What can you do to increase student Voice at your school? In your home?

POWERFUL EDUCATOR™

CONCLUSION

NINE YEARS AGO, I WENT back to Ethiopia for the first time since my family fled. As we were driving through the countryside in my home province, I took this picture of a young girl. Take a moment and tell me what you see.

This photo has always saddened me. I wonder if like my mother, this young girl will not have a school to attend. She looks about six years old and her job is to watch those massive oxen from dawn to dusk. Were she in the United States, she might already know how to read. She might have limitless growth opportunities. Music. Sports. Education.

Earlier this year, I sat on a plane next to a professional photographer. He showed me some of his favorite photos. I had the picture of the girl on my computer and showed it to him. I also shared how I felt.

Here's what he said, "I completely disagree with you. I see a girl so strong, she can command oxen ten times her size with just a small stick. I see a girl so confident, she can walk down the cliff before her and not flinch. I see a leader."

I was more than a bit ashamed. Here I was, after all my years in education, putting boxes around this young girl from my homeland, discounting her power and judging her entire future based on one photo. But she is far more powerful than I know.

Powerful Educator

I WROTE THIS BOOK BECAUSE you do the same thing to yourself. As an educator, as a parent, as a mentor, as a volunteer, *you discount your own power.*

Life wears you down; the politics at your school beat you up; your kids tire you out. And you get to the point where it's easier to just give in.

You think, *"Hey, let me just get through this year. I'm not accomplishing much anyway."* You think, *"These kids don't listen to me. Why am I working so hard?"* You think, *"Why rock the boat when I get attacked every time?"*

You paint a picture of yourself as powerless, as mediocre when it comes to our youth.

I disagree. I see a Powerful Educator. You were born to inspire and lead. Without you, our youth cannot rise to their rightful place as heroes. They cannot lead our world forward.

I have spent fifteen years meeting Powerful Educators like you. You are the backbone of everything, and I mean *everything*, that is good about education. I want to thank you for helping me see your five greatest Powers.

1. **Press Your Turbo Button**
2. **Relate with Heart**
3. **Speak Success Mindsets**
4. **Push for Skill**
5. **Champion Voice**

I hope I meet you at your school someday. Better yet, I hope we bump into each other at an airport.

If you can tell me how you've used your Five Powers, I'll buy you a sandwich.

For Powerful Educator Staff Workshops and Professional Development, visit **MawiLearning.com**.

POWERFUL EDUCATOR™

APPENDIX A
Works Referenced

Bridgeland, John, Mary Bruce, and Arya Hariharan. The Missing Piece: A National Teacher Survey on How Social and Emotional Learning Can Empower Children and Transform Schools. Rep. 16 Sept. 2013. Civic Enterprises, Hart Research Associates, Collaborative for Academic, Social and Emotional Learning (CASEL).

Buddin, Richard and Gema Zamarro. What Teacher Characteristics Affect Student Achievement? Findings from Los Angeles Public Schools. Santa Monica, CA: RAND Corporation, 2010.

Campbell, Joseph. *The Hero with a Thousand Faces*. Princeton, NJ: Princeton UP, 1968.

Carnegie, Dale. *How to Win Friends and Influence People*. New York: Simon and Schuster, 1981.

Covey, Stephen R. *The Seven Habits of Highly Effective People: Restoring the Character Ethic*. New York: Simon and Schuster, 1989.

Duncan, Arne. "A Call to Teaching: Secretary Arne Duncan's Remarks at The Rotunda at the University of Virginia." Archived: A Call to Teaching: Secretary Arne Duncan's Remarks at The Rotunda at the University of Virginia. 09 Oct. 2009. U.S Department of Education.

Farrington, Camille A., Melissa Roderick, Elaine Allensworth, Jenny Nagaoka, Tasha Seneca Keyes, David W. Johnson, and Nicole O. Beechum. <u>Teaching Adolescents To Become Learners: The Role of Noncognitive Factors in Shaping School Performance: A Critical Literature Review</u>. Rep. June 2012. The University of Chicago Consortium on Chicago School Research, Lumina Foundation, Raikes Foundation.

Gershoff, Elizabeth Thompson. "Corporal Punishment by Parents and Associated Child Behaviors and Experiences: A Meta-analytic and Theoretical Review."*Psychological Bulletin* 128.4 (2002): 539-79.

Holland, Kelley. "Why Johnny Can't Write, and Why Employers Are Mad." *NBC News*. National Broadcasting Company, 11 Nov. 2013. Web.

Jeynes, William H. "Parental Involvement and Student Achievement: A Meta-Analysis/Family Involvement Research Digests /Publications Series/Publications & Resources/HFRP - Harvard Family Research Project." <u>Parental Involvement and Student Achievement: A Meta-Analysis</u>. Dec. 2005. Harvard Family Research Project.

MacCann, Carolyn, Angela Lee Duckworth, and Richard D. Rogers. "Empirical Identification of the major facets of Conscientiousness." <u>Learning and Individual Differences</u> 19 (2009): 451-58. <u>Elsevier</u>. 09 Mar. 2009.

Neff, Linda S. "Lev Vygotsky and Social Learning Theories." *Lev Vygotsky and Social Learning Theories*. Northern Arizona University, n.d. Web.

Nord, Christine W., and Jerry West. <u>Fathers' and Mothers' Involvement in Their Children's Schools by Family Type and Resident Status</u>. 07 May 2001. U.S. Department of Education Office of Education Research and Improvement.

Seligman, Martin E. P., Karen Reivich, Lisa Jaycox, and Jane Gillham. <u>The Optimistic Child: A Proven Program to Safeguard Children Against Depression and Build Lifelong Resilience</u>. Boston: Houghton Mifflin Co., 2007.

POWERFUL EDUCATOR™

────────────────────APPENDIX B
Works Synthesized by Powerful Educator

Power 1: Press Your Turbo Button

BANDURA, ALBERT. "Social Cognitive Theory: An Agentic Perspective." <u>Annual Review of Psychology</u> 52 (2001): 1-26.

People's perception of their own control over their life is a key factor in their ability to act. In this study, psychologist Albert Bandura explores how self-efficacy, or an individual's perception of their ability to learn, and organize and execute goals, dictates their ability to take action. He evaluates how self-efficacy and self-agency work with each other in positive or negative ways in an increasingly complex world.

DUCKWORTH, ANGELA L., CHRISTOPHER PETERSON, MICHAEL D. MATTHEWS, AND DENNIS R. KELLY. "Grit: Perseverance and passion for long-term goals." <u>Journal of Personality and Social Psychology</u> 92 (2007): 1087-101.

In "Grit: Perseverance and passion for long-term goals", researchers test the hypothesis that Grit, defined as the ability to act with perseverance and passion for long-term goals, is a success factor in educational attainment, class retention and student ranking. They determined that Grit was a success factor over and beyond that of IQ and conscientiousness in a study of two classes of United States Military Academy West Point Cadets and in ranking in the National Spelling Bee. This suggests that "the achievement of difficult goals entails not only talent but also the sustained and focused application of talent over time."

DUCKWORTH, ANGELA L., AND MARTIN E.P. SELIGMAN. "Self-Discipline Outdoes IQ in Predicting Academic Performance of Adolescents." Psychological Science 16 (2005): 939-44.

This study attempted to distinguish what separates top students from others in terms of academic success. Building on previous studies, Duckworth and Seligman measured 164 eighth graders' self-discipline and self-control. They discovered that "Self-discipline measured in the fall accounted for more than twice as much variance as IQ in final grades, high school selection, school attendance, hours spent doing homework, hours spent watching television (inversely), and the time of day students began their homework." Ultimately they concluded that one of the major factors for students failing to meet their potential was a lack of self-discipline.

Power 2: Relate With Heart

KLEM, ADENA M., AND JAMES P. CONNELL. "Relationships Matter: Linking Teacher Support to Student Engagement and Achievement." Journal of School Health 74 (2004): 262-73.

This study synthesized and examined research on the effects of teacher-student relationships on student engagement. It found that teacher support, as reported by students and teachers, and characterized by caring, personal relationships between teachers and students, is vital to student engagement. Students that perceived their teachers as creating a caring, supportive environment with well-defined structure and fair, clear expectations were more likely to report high engagement in schools. Student engagement was found to have an impact on grades and test scores. The researchers found that this pattern held true for both elementary and middle school students.

SIMON, BETH S. "Family Involvement in High School: Predictors and Effects." <u>National Association of Secondary School Principals Bulletin</u> 85 (2001): 8-19.

In this study, reports from over 11,000 high school principals and parents of high school students were analyzed to better understand high school, community and parent partnerships. The study found that regardless of student prior achievement, status or background, parental involvement greatly impacted student grades, course credits completed, attendance, behavior, and school preparedness. Furthermore, they found that parental involvement increased when solicited and guided by educators.

WENTZEL, KATHRYN R. "Social relationships and motivation in middle school: The role of parents, teachers, and peers." <u>Journal of Educational Psychology</u> 90 (1998): 202-09.

167 sixth graders were surveyed in this study to understand the impact of teacher, peer and parental involvement in shaping adolescents' motivation at school (social goal pursuit, academic goal orientations and school/class related interests). Researchers found that peer involvement was a strong indicator for pro-social motivation. They found that teacher involvement was an indicator for both social goal pursuit and school/class related interests, while parents proved to be a strong indicator for school/class in-

terests and academic goal orientations. The study also acknowledged the role of peers and parents in decreasing emotional distress, thereby indirectly increasing school interest.

Chapter 3: Speak Success Mindsets

DWECK, CAROL S. <u>Mindset: The New Psychology of Success</u>. New York: Random House, 2006.

In this ground-breaking book, Stanford psychologist and researcher Carol Dweck synthesizes decades of research on what fosters success. Dweck reveals that it's not our talent or ability that makes us successful, but whether we approach life with a fixed or growth mindset. She emphasizes that a growth mindset is an integral part of motivating our children and ourselves to reach our goals. She further links this idea with academic success for students and demonstrates that a growth mindset is key for developing a foundation of resilience and a future of achievement.

DWECK, CAROL S., GREGORY M. WALTON, AND GEOFFREY L. COHEN. <u>Academic tenacity: Mindset and skills that promote long-term learning</u>. Paper. 2011. The Gates Foundation.

In this Gates Foundation study, Stanford University researcher and psychologist Carol Dweck partners with Drs. Gregory Walton and Geoffrey Cohen to examine how teaching motivation and mindset skills can improve academic success for students. Specifically, the authors examine how non-cognitive skills such as academic tenacity, self-regulation, self-efficacy, a sense of belonging, grit and having long term goals affect student success. The authors demonstrate that targeting these non-cognitive factors can play a larger role in student success than the traditional focus on academic or instructional reforms.

YEAGER, DAVID S., AND CAROL S. DWECK. "Mindsets That Promote Resilience: When Students Believe That Personal Characteristics Can Be Developed." Educational Psychologist 47 (2012): 302-14. Educational Psychologist. 19 Oct. 2012.

Drs. David Yeager and Carol Dweck review research on the impact of students' mindsets on their resilience in the face of academic and social challenges. They contrast the difference between students that are taught or believe that academic success and intellectual prowess can be gained through effort versus students that believe it is fixed. They conclude that students that believe it can be developed show higher achievement through difficult transitions and greater course completion in complex math courses. They also examine new research that examines whether or not teaching that social attributes can be developed can lower aggression and stress in response to bullying, resulting in increased school success. It concludes with a discussion of what educators can do to help students develop these mindsets.

SHECHTMAN, NICOLE, ANGELA H. DEBARGER, CAROLYN DORNSIFE, SOREN ROSIER, AND LOUISE YARNALL. Promoting Grit, Tenacity, and Perseverance: Critical Factors for Success in the 21st Century. Rep. 14 Feb. 2013. U.S. Department of Education Office of Educational Technology, Center for Technology in Learning, SRI International.

This massive report asks: how can we prepare our children and adolescents to thrive in the 21st century? To answer that question, researchers looked at a core set of non-cognitive skills: grit, tenacity and perseverance.

They examined what they are, how they can be measured, what impact they have and what learning environments are the most conducive to producing them. The report presents an exhaustive review of current literature on the subject as well as interviews with researchers and thought leaders in this area. What they found is that students can develop the psychological resources that promote grit, tenacity and perseverance. They discovered that sociocultural factors play a large role in the implementation of programming and that rigorous, supportive learning environments are key to developing growth mindsets.

Chapter 4: Push for Skill

DUCKWORTH, ANGELA L., HEIDI GRANT, BENJAMIN LOEW, GABRIELE OETTINGEN, AND PETER M. GOLL-WITZER. "Self regulation strategies improve self discipline in adolescents: Benefits of mental contrasting and implementation intentions." Educational Psychology: An International Journal of Experimental Educational Psychology 31 (2011): 17-26.

This study examines the struggle adolescents face in setting and striving for goals that require prolonged self-discipline. It examines a concept they term "mental contrasting", a cognitive process by which adults contrast a desired future outcome with present relevant obstacles and "implementation intentions", cognitive strategy that determines what action will be taken when an opportunity relevant to achieve their goal arises. Researchers test the effects of combining mental contrasting with implementation intentions on goal implementation with adolescents, particu-

larly a set of 62 high school students preparing to take a test. They found that students taught the mental contrasting and implementation intention skills prepared much more successfully for the test, indicating the merit of teaching students these self-regulatory skills.

SELIGMAN, MARTIN E. P., KAREN REIVICH, LISA JAYCOX, AND JANE GILLHAM. The Optimistic Child: A Proven Program to Safeguard Children Against Depression and Build Lifelong Resilience. Boston: Houghton Mifflin Co., 2007.

In his book, "The Optimistic Child", University of Pennsylvania researcher Dr. Martin Seligman examines the concept of building confidence in children. By studying over 100,000 children, Seligman concludes that the self-esteem movement has actually harmed many kids. He concludes that the best way to help children achieve is to help them build real skills and praise growth, rather than praise fixed qualities.

TOUGH, PAUL. How Children Succeed: Grit, Curiosity, and the Hidden Power of Character. Boston: Houghton Mifflin Harcourt, 2012.

In author Paul Tough's "How Children Succeed: Grit, Curiosity, and the Hidden Power of Character", Tough interrogates the traditional belief that cognitive skills such as verbal acuity, mathematical ability and the ability to detect patterns that are the best indicators of academic and future success. By synthesizing literature and research in this area, Tough shows that IQ based indications have been disproven as a definitive predictor for future success. Increasingly, non-cognitive skills such as perseverance, conscientiousness, optimism, curiosity and self-discipline are proving to be better indicators for achievement. Tough argues that teachers need to build these skills while engaging student curiosity to promote academic success.

ZINS, JOSEPH E., ROGER P. WEISSBERG, MARGARET C. WANG, AND HERBERT J. WALBERG. Building academic success on social and emotional learning: What does the research say? New York: Teachers College P, 2004.

In this book, researchers examine the relationship between academic success and social emotional learning skills. By examining current literature and synthesizing various studies, they make a compelling case that social emotional learning interventions work to increase student success. Specifically, they point to increased academic success for students with strong non-cognitive skills, increased student focus and motivation, a strengthening of the relationship between teachers and their students and increased student confidence and success.

Chapter 5: Champion Voice

MAHONEY, JOSEPH L., AND ROBERT B. CAIRNS. "Do Extracurricular Activities Protect against Early School Dropout?" *Developmental Psychology* 33.2 (1997): 241-53.

This study followed 392 adolescents from 7-12th grade to see if early participation in extracurricular activities had any effect on dropout rates. Dropout was considered failure to complete 11th grade. Researchers found that students deemed "at risk" who participated in extracurricular activities showed markedly lower dropout rates than their peers who did not participate in extracurricular activities.

DAVALOS, D. B., E. L. CHAVEZ, AND R. J. GUARDIOLA. "The

Effects of Extracurricular Activity, Ethnic Identification, and Perception of School on Student Dropout Rates." *Hispanic Journal of Behavioral Sciences* 21.1 (1999): 61-77.

In this article, researchers examined the relationship between participation in an extracurricular activity and dropout rates for Mexican Americans and White Non-Hispanics. It also looked at the level of student ethnic identification and school perception. They found that students that reported engagement in one or more extra-curricular activities were 2.30 times more likely to be enrolled in school than those reporting no engagement in extracurricular activities.

MEZUK, BRIANA. "Urban Debate and High School Educational Outcomes for African American Males: The Case of the Chicago Debate League." *The Journal of Negro Education* 78.3 (2009): 290-304. Print.

This article synthesizes one particular instance of championing student voice. This study analyzed whether or not participation by African American males in the Chicago Debate League had any effect on scholastic success and dropout rates. Mezuk analyzed data from 1997 to 2006 and found that students who participated in Chicago Debate League were 70% more likely to graduate and three times less likely to drop out than students who did not compete in the league.

POWERFUL EDUCATOR™

APPENDIX C
Going Around the Wheel

WHAT DOES IT LOOK LIKE to help a student go around the Action Wheel? How do you, as an educator or parent, use this tool to build real skill in children? We want to provide you with one specific example of going around The Action Wheel.

1. **Explore:** Pick a character quality or skill and explain it to a student. Even better, have the student explain it to you.
2. **Plan:** Help the student make a plan of how they will use that quality in their own life in the coming week.
3. **Act:** Track with the student as they implement the character quality.
4. **Reflect:** Debrief with the student, along with the other students.

Action Wheel Example: Initiative

IN THIS EXAMPLE, STUDENTS explore the concept of taking initiative.

1. Explore

In the Explore phase of initiative, you want students to understand what initiative is and why it matters. You can present examples of initiative through stories, famous persons, or guest speakers.

In Charisse's school, her teacher had them break into partner groups after reading a story about a boy who raised money for an orphanage in Thailand. They discussed what it meant to take initiative and how they might take initiative in their own lives.

2. Plan

In the Plan phase, you help your students identify how they will take initiative. To help students brainstorm, you can ask students to list some challenges, interests and dreams.

Charisse's teacher had them each list their challenges, interests and dreams. Charisse immediately listed running the mile as a challenge as she dreaded it every year. She listed her interests as being a good student, listening to music and cooking. Lastly, she wrote down that her dream was to be a nurse in the Army, like her aunt.

Charisse decided to tackle her challenge, running the mile. When planning her action, Charisse's teacher had her use the MAD Goals framework. The goal must be Measurable, Attainable, and Deadline-driven. Charisse agreed to practice five days a week, going a little bit farther each day, in the month leading up to the mile run at school.

3. Act

During the Action phase, teachers support students in taking their actions. This can be done by meeting with them for 5 minutes once a week, by having them record their progress in a journal, or by having students motivate each other with weekly check ins.

Charisse chose to keep track in a journal. Each day she placed a check next to the date to indicate whether or not she ran. She also recorded the amount of time she had run without stopping. Her teacher checked it every week. When she noticed that Charisse had missed running for 3 days in a row, she checked in with her. Charisse explained that her mom had been sick at the beginning and now she felt that she had missed too many days to continue. Her teacher encouraged her to pick up where she left off and monitored closely for a couple of days.

When the day of the mile run came, Charisse completed the mile run in 12 minutes and 13 seconds without walking!

4. Reflect

During the Reflection phase, students process what they have learned about Initiative. Teachers can facilitate classroom discussion and setup small group activities.

Charisse's teacher had a party for the class for completing their initiatives. She asked them to answer this question: "When were you the most tempted to give up and what helped you to keep going?" Charisse shared that when she missed so many days of running, she felt like she had already failed. For her, the most important thing was hearing that she could start again and that stalling didn't mean failing.

Mawi Learning's Mental Karate program takes students through five loops of the Action Wheel with the following character principles: Initiative, Contribution, Discipline, Courage, and Awareness. You can learn more at **MentalKarate.com**.

APPENDIX D
Let Your Voice Be Heard!

Student Service Projects with Mawi Learning's Leadership Skills Course

OVER THE LAST YEAR, STUDENTS in the Florida Virtual School Mawi Learning Leadership Class have led over 1,000 service projects. Students chose, planned, and implemented their service projects as the culmination of their leadership training.

This appendix provides additional information about how students are using their Voice, and a sample of those projects. How can your students exercise their Voice through service?

WHO ARE THEY SERVING?
The three biggest impact areas were the environment, youth, and fundraising.

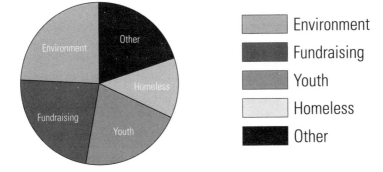

- Environment
- Fundraising
- Youth
- Homeless
- Other

ATHLETIC DEPARTMENT FUNDRAISER: Miguel completed his service project through raising money for his school's athletic department. Miguel recognized that their equipment and uniforms needed some updating, so he and his teammates asked the principal for permission to fundraise. They organized a bake sale and promoted it by posting flyers around their school. Miguel organized a consistent fundraising schedule so that his teammates were able to participate. On average, the team raised about $300/week and recently reached their overall goal of $5,000. Their fundraiser gained so much community attention, they were able to attract a local sponsor and will be wearing their new uniforms this fall!

COMMUNITY GARDEN: Andre started a community garden for a group of students who wanted to improve their lives after committing misdemeanor crimes. Each group member committed to take some time each week to tend to the garden's fruits and vegetables. When the fruits and vegetables were finished growing, the group donated them to a local church.

PROMDRESS.COM: Andrea started a website where girls could go to find gently used Prom dresses. She felt that buying a Prom dress can be very expensive and she didn't want anyone to miss out on an important night because they couldn't afford a nice dress. Girls who donated their dresses could go on the website and post a picture, and those in need were able to go on the site and look for one they liked.

HIGH SCHOOL BAND FUNDRAISER: Vlad is a member of his high school band. After some time, Vlad realized that some of his fellow members were having trouble paying their band fees, so he decided to help. Vlad organized a car wash to raise money so that all members could stay in the band. He was able to get members of the band and color guard to help him volunteer at the car wash and they raised $700 which was $200 over his original goal.

UNICEF: Jessica helped fundraise for a global program called UNICEF, where the money she raised went toward the prevention of neonatal and maternal tetanus in third world countries. $1.80 could help one mother and child, but Jessica knew she wanted to make a big impact, so she held a bake sale, a raffle, a "walk for the cure," and sold carnations to raise the money. In the end, Jessica raised $1,172.47 which impacted a total of 651 lives.

KEEP THE PARK: Jason heard about a park in his community that officials were considering shutting down. For his service project, Jason acted as community advocate, educating community members about the park community officials wanted to close. He gained support from community members and had a group accompany him to the district office where they were able to convince officials not to knock down their park.

BILINGUAL HOSPITAL VOLUNTEER: Rosa wanted to complete her service project by volunteering at a local hospital. At first, she was just helping out at the front desk but she soon realized that the hospital staff could use one of her very important skills.

Rosa is bilingual, so she helped hospital staff communicate with patients which resulted in Rosa spending some one-on-one time with patients. Rosa made a big impact on the patients she visited and on the staff who benefited from her ability to communicate more effectively with patients.

RECYCLING EDUCATION: Ashley saw a need for education in her community, specifically on the topic of recycling. Ashley posted educational flyers on recycling around her town. The flyers highlighted why recycling is important to the environment and listed reasons why it should be important to the community members on a personal level. Ashley noticed that after her flyers went up, more people in her neighborhood started using their recycling bins more often and she feels confident that her community education effort had a great impact on her community!

ABOUT MAWI

A REFUGEE TURNED HARVARD GRADUATE, Mawi Asgedom has written eight books that are used by school districts across the world. Mawi has spoken to over 1,000,000 students and trained educators at many leading conferences. Media outlets such as The Oprah Winfrey Show, *The Chicago Tribune, Harvard Magazine,* and *ESSENCE* have recognized Mawi for his impact.

Mawi Learning provides educators with books, courses, and professional development that increase the academic, career, and life opportunities of youth. **You can get deeper Powerful Educator training for your staff by taking the Powerful Educator online course, created in partnership with Mindset Works.**

Visit MawiLearning.com to learn more.

Want to increase your power even more?

Take the Powerful Educator Online Course with your team!

You will:

- Learn directly from Dr. Carol Dweck on how to build a Growth Mindset
- Create actionable lessons and plans for classroom and school culture transformation
- Have access to over 60 training videos from Mawi and Powerful Educators around the world

Email **courses@MawiLearning.com** to learn more